This book is a must-read for all ... desperation to see people throughout th... lives to Jesus. It's honest about the cu... about the future and laced with Scriptu... of how powerfully the Lord moves. We ... need to pray our par... in witnessing in this season in the UK, and I wholeheartedly recommend this book as a wonderful tool to get us started.

GAVIN CALVER
CEO of Evangelical Alliance

This book came as a surprise to me as I thought I would be reading the 'how to's of evangelism and a prodding to "get out there and do it', but it's not like that at all! It is a brief, all-encompassing read which deals with our own salvation and discipleship as well as helping us theologically with the bigger picture and our inheritance in Christ. Only then does Mike encourage us in our witnessing to others. I enjoyed reading it very much and felt really stirred by it. Read it, it will do you good!

ANGELA KEMM
Prophetic Evangelist, City Church Cambridge & Relational Mission

As much-needed as this kind of encouragement ever is, Mike's book reminds us of the wonderful truths that we as Christians have been swept into, of the great need people have for Christ, and then shows us what it looks like to be witnesses for Him, partnering with God Himself – all in a way that gets us thinking, "Even I can do that!" Stirring, emboldening and easy-to-grasp, I'd love to see this in the hands of every Christian.

STEVE DUNN
Lead Elder, The Beacon Church Herne Bay

EVERYONE A WITNESS

Published by Relational Mission

Jubilee Family Centre, Norwich Road, Aylsham, Norfolk, NR11 6JG, UK

www.relationalmission.com

ISBN 978-1-9162781-5-8

Acknowledgements

Scripture quotations are from The ESV® Bible (The Holy Bible, English Standard Version®), copyright © 2001 by Crossway, a publishing ministry of Good News Publishers. Used by permission. All rights reserved.

Scripture quotations taken from the Amplified® Bible (AMPC), Copyright © 1954, 1958, 1962, 1964, 1965, 1987 by The Lockman Foundation Used by permission. www.lockman.org

A catalogue record of this book is available from the British Library

Cover Design by Daniel Goodman

Typeset in Adobe Garamond Pro

EVERYONE A WITNESS

By Mike Betts

Published by *Relational Mission*

ACKNOWLEDGEMENTS

Everyone a Witness is the latest in a series of books flowing from the themes contained within the book *Relational Mission – A Way of Life*.

My aim is to write readable, accessible and concise books that are hopefully challenging, stimulating and empowering for fellow followers of Christ.

The Christian life is very simple but it is not easy. My hope and prayer as you explore this book and maybe some of the others is that the simplicity of our faith will empower and disentangle us from all hindrances, that we might "bear much fruit"[1] for the glory of God.

I want to say a massive thank you to a number of people without whom writing and releasing this book simply would not have been possible. Firstly, Phil Whittall for his outstanding editorial gifts. He has helped keep the content

---

[1] John 15:8.

crisp and true to the intended simple message of 'everyone a witness'.

Then a whole number of other dear friends from across the *Relational Mission* family of churches, namely; Annice Green, Steve Dunn, Penny Taylor, Daniel Goodman and Poppy Balding, who have helped with proofreading, cover design, preparing content and sourcing quotes. My thanks and appreciation to each and every one.

Finally, this book is dedicated to pastor Malcolm Pears through whom I came to know Christ.

CONTENTS

CONTENTS

FOREWORD

Four years ago, I was standing in a museum at Ginosar on the shore of Lake Galilee. There I marvelled at a wonderfully preserved first century Jewish fishing boat. Discovered in 1986, no one knows if Jesus ever sat in it, or preached from it, but being up close and personal took me back in time to the start of Mark's gospel.

Peter and Andrew made their living as fishermen in such a boat on the same lake. Mark's gospel is the earliest we have. As we begin to read, we see that Jesus is about to speak the first recorded words we hear from Him. Imagine the young rabbi approaching the brothers. (Perhaps James and John, the sons of Zebedee, are looking on from a distance.) Jesus clears His throat and confidently says to Peter and Andrew: "Come, follow me and I will make you fishers of men."[2]

---

[2] Mark 1:17.

What would Peter and Andrew have thought of this invitation? Clearly following Jesus and becoming a "fisher of men" were linked. Jesus seems to think that "follow me" and being a "fisher of men" were part of the same deal. Not two different things, but one big thing, one big journey, one big adventure.

By contrast, "Come follow me" sounds like what we Christians call discipleship. And, to our ears, fishing for men and women sounds like something different – what we call evangelism. But none of Jesus' early followers would have understood that distinction. Jesus taught His followers while they were walking to the next outreach location. All the discipleship they received from Jesus was in the context of mission. Asking one of Jesus' twelve disciples to describe evangelism would have been like asking a fish to describe water. The only kind of Christianity that existed on Earth was missional.

Today, by contrast, we have "Come follow me" specialists who are really good at discipleship, and we also have a much smaller number of maverick, extrovert 'fishers of men'. The common perception being that "I'd need a personality transplant to become one of them." Yet Jesus never required Peter and Andrew to undergo a personality transplant. How did we ever divorce two things which Jesus saw as one thing? Isn't it time to revisit the idea that "What God has joined together, let no man cast asunder."[3]

Mike Betts' book is timely. Because it's time to reverse the great divorce. Mike's book goes back to the original Jesus, in the actual Bible. You and I blundered when we divorced discipleship from evangelism. Mike Betts shows that the original plan was 'everyone a witness'.

I read this book in one sitting yesterday evening. Earlier the same day, I heard the shocking news that one of the most successful and best known Christian leaders in the UK had left the ministry he founded. Why? Because he had become so concerned about the need for everyone to become a witness! He's left his world famous ministry behind to develop an app that works along the following lines:

Step 1: Tell someone you work with or someone you know that you are a Christian.

---

[3] Mark 10:9.

Step 2: Do life with them. That is to say: do something with them, whether it's inviting them over for dinner or playing a game or watching a game with them. Just do something normal with them.

Step 3: Share Jesus. Actually talk about Jesus.

What if every Christian did this? What if everyone was a witness? What if it could actually be fun? What if this is normal Christianity? What if this is how Jesus always designed and envisaged the whole thing working? What if this is how the great commission will be fulfilled? What if this is how every tribe and tongue will be reached? What if this simple idea will actually bring about the return of Jesus Christ to Earth? What if "Come follow me and I will make you a fisher of men" is just as good for us as it would have been good for us if Jesus had said "Come follow me and I will make you a cup of tea." It's the same Jesus making the invitation. The same Jesus who prioritised us and chose us when He was under pressure in the Garden of Gethsemane. What if the whole Christian life is actually supposed to be an adventure that faces outwards?

The church has faced plagues and pandemics before and triumphed through them. Communism was a massive global attempt to impose atheism, but the church triumphed. Even today there are 100 million Christians in China.

In the upper room, in Jerusalem, after the resurrection, there were only 120 believers. And yet within 300 years, the Roman Empire was Christian. Even the Emperor was a Christian. And what's even more stunning about that is that for most of the time from 33 AD until 313 AD, Christianity was illegal.

How did the church grow? Well it was started by someone who said "Come follow me and I will make you fishers of men." How come there are 100 million Christians in China? Well the church was started by someone who said "Come follow me and I will make you fishers of men."

The Bible talks about two things that will last forever:

1. The Word of God, and

2. People, who will live forever either in heaven or in hell.

Jesus said in Matthew 7:22 that He will be the judge on that judgement day. And that everyone's eternal destiny will hinge on whether or not they knew Jesus in this life.

What an amazingly important message we have been given.

Robert Woodruff was president of Coca-Cola from 1923 to 1955, and he was an outstanding visionary leader. His vision was that one day in the future no one on Earth would die without first, at some point in their life, having tasted Coca-Cola. Back then most people in South America, in Africa and Asia had heard of Coca-Cola, but most had never tasted it. His vision was that everyone should get to taste Coca-Cola at least once before they died.

We want people to taste the real thing. Most people living near us have heard the name of Jesus. We want people to taste the real Jesus. I know you want that. So read on. Let Mike take you there.

ADRIAN HOLLOWAY

The John 3:16 Trust

www.adrianholloway.com

The Beacon Church, Camberley

www.beaconchurch.co.uk

1
A WELSH ROCK POOL
THERE IS LIFE BUT THERE IS MORE

When I was at High School, we went on a field trip to the Welsh coast. On a day when it wasn't raining, we spent our time exploring the rock pools along the beautiful craggy coastline. Wandering from pool to pool, peering in, we were captivated by these tiny worlds of vibrant colour – seaweeds and flora dancing in the gentle swirl of the water – and spotting crabs, shrimps and limpets. This simple act of observing, listing and recording this abundance of life, as we hopped from pool to pool, has for some reason stuck in my memory.

Fascinating as the rock pools were, they offered only a very limited perspective of 'sea life'. Why? The tide was out. When the tide is in, the rock pools disappear – they are absorbed into a much bigger ocean of life. Imagine thinking rock pools are all that there is to sea life, which you might do if you didn't realise that the tide will inevitably bring the waves back over the rocks! When the tide comes in everything changes. The shoreline looks different, the rocks and cliffs, which look fixed and unchanging, get shaped as mighty waves crash in. And under the surface an abundance of creatures, and shoals of fish too big for a rock pool now swim in the deep waters.

At the time of writing I have just turned 60. I have been a Christian since roughly the age of 17. Every year of my life, in the UK where I live and across the westernised world, I have only seen the church decline. This decline has been both numerical and in terms of societal influence. It is as though the tide of Christianity has gone out further and further, year after year. Fewer people are coming to Christ, and more are drifting away. The gospel of "grace alone, by faith alone, in Christ alone" has been either abandoned entirely or it has been watered down. Christian life seems increasingly like another accessory in a spiritual supermarket. Nominalism is on the rise and it is rare to hear of radical costly decisions being made by those turning to Christ or indeed by those living for Christ. The cost of following Christ and the clarity, conviction and distinctiveness of the Christian church is in danger of being lost.

Is there anything that marks us out as different from the world around us? Stories of Jesus helping us with needs are plentiful and we praise God for those, but stories of Jesus convicting us of ungodly attitudes and moving us to surrender areas of our lives to Him seem less common. The gospel has been challenged from both inside and outside of the church. The influence of the Christian faith in society has diminished slowly, year by year. I have never had a year of my life when I haven't felt that the tide has been going out.

Many of the nations in the westernised world especially are now in a sorry spiritual state of affairs. There are small pockets of church life that look and feel very much like the rock pools I described. Maybe, as you read this, you are thinking, "Hey Mike, come and see what is going on in our church. God is moving in great ways. Our church is seeing lots of people come to Christ. We have outgrown our building twice now." Or something similar.

Such reports are truly heart-warming and they do ignite hope and lift the spirit. There are thankfully many such 'rock pool' reports of abundant life, and if, like the rock pools, we spent the day exploring these local church expressions, we would find them full of beauty and life, and with a whole ecosystem of spiritual abundance even. But, dear friends, however good it is in your church it is still a rock pool and the tide is still out.

This can't be the sum of it. Surely God has more on His heart? Are there not promises of more in the Scriptures? How does this reflection make you feel? Whatever you do, don't stop reading now, thinking "This is depressing", because there is cause for great hope. Anyone who is familiar with the sea knows that when the tide is out you can be sure it will eventually come in again. Well, "first the natural then the spiritual"[4]. Paul points out that we can learn lessons about how God acts and moves by looking at what He has created and how it functions. Tides go out but they also come in!

In the West, we do see beautiful surges of God's Spirit washing over the church, bringing fresh life and vibrancy to

----

[4] 1 Corinthians 15:46.

4

the rock pool coast of Christianity. They remind us the incoming tide is indeed on its way.

Here is a story from my friend Clyde Thomas of what the Holy Spirit did in Victory Church, Cwmbran, Wales during 2013:

> *I remember Wednesday night, 10th April 2013 very well. I had only been on the leadership at Victory Church for probably two months then. Victory Church had been planted out of a rehabilitation home and had a deep love for the poor and for the broken. That formed a foundation for this incredible desire to reach lost and broken people and to see them restored, refreshed and built back up.*
>
> *A couple of weeks before that particular Wednesday, there was such a sense of excitement – a sense of real expectation – in the meetings. There were maybe 50-60 people gathered for this prayer gathering on Wednesday night, 10th April 2013. The preacher was speaking from the book of Esther and as he got to the end of the message it was as if a strong sense of the presence of God entered the room and fell on the place.*
>
> *During the next 10-15 minutes, as people were receiving prayer, that sense of presence seemed to intensify*

to the point that a gentleman who was in a wheelchair literally jumped up and carried his wheelchair above his head! Our meetings are in an old warehouse and it's quite a big space and this man actually ran 2-3 laps around the auditorium. This gentleman was completely healed from that night.

Well, I guess the sense of anticipation that followed that – this sense that God can do anything, God can do the impossible – just built and grew each night. For the next six months or so we met nightly, just having the Friday off, and I was privileged to be involved in a lot of that ministry as well. A team of us, four or five of us, were involved in preaching ministry and prayer ministry amidst that time. It was weird because during those months, we didn't seem to get tired. It was like we were sustained. Our energy levels were sustained and although we were exerting a lot of energy meeting after meeting, night after night, and up to 100,000 people visiting in from around the world, people travelling in during the daytimes, spending time with them, praying with them and then doing meetings in the evening, it was like a supernatural energy was upon us. We were just refreshed.

But after about seven months I remember having a distinct feeling that though this was still amazing, something had shifted. It wasn't quite the same. I think that was God just moving away from that time of refreshing. But during that time, we saw some amazing things.

We saw one family who were sitting in their home in Cwmbran – I think it was two kids, if I remember rightly, and a mum and dad – they actually had this incredible sense that they should come up to the church. They had not been to church before and the dad turned the TV off in the house and basically turned up at the church and as they got into the car park they basically wept uncontrollably. They repented of their sin and were saved by the time they got to the front door of the church.

One gentleman came forward and he had a hearing aid on, and he had his arm in a sling and he had a growth on his belly area. I watched with my own eyes the growth disappear. And the man said "Well look, if God can do that… ', so he took his hearing aid off! Well, his ear popped open and he could hear. So then he took his sling off too and his arm was healed.

People were becoming Christians every single night. Sometimes 15, 20, 30 people became a Christian. People were getting saved and it was just incredible.

One day the postman came in to deliver the mail, as postmen do. He was overtaken by the sense of the presence

*of God. He received prayer in the foyer of the church. It
really was an unexpected season, an incredible season.*

*In reflection, it teaches us that God really is the God of
the impossible and when you're in it you don't realise just
how special it is. I sometimes look back and think: What
was that? How did that even happen? How do we
experience that again? And by God's grace He's continued
to pour His Spirit in our gatherings, and we see people
saved and rescued, but I just long for that more intense
sense of God's presence again. That sense of "God is in the
room, God is with us, He is right in the room with us."
They are really special times.*

What do you think, having read what Clyde had to say? It
makes me look to the horizon and wonder, "Is the tide finally
turning?"

The low-tide nature of gospel fruitfulness that the western
world currently experiences is far from the whole story. In
many areas of the world, especially in the global South and
East the tide is most definitely in and rising. There many know
nothing of 'rock pools'. They live in the days of great tidal
surges of seeing God at work. When I talk to dear friends I
partner with, in places such as Africa and the Middle East, it

is not uncommon to hear reports of churches consistently thriving despite great adversity caused by famine, poverty, and unstable or repressive political government. Often, in spite of such harsh daily realities, significant numbers of people are coming to Christ resulting in increased church planting.

This is my friend J sharing a story from Syria:

My dad's name is Abraham, and he is a leader, and man of God. I remember in the midst of the war, when we were living there, it was a very difficult time. There was a lot of hardship, missiles, bullets, scary moments, nieces and nephews in tears, and, when the battles erupted, people hiding in their houses. It was a difficult time. To be able to go in and out of Syria at that time, we had to get special documents. To get those documents we had to travel to another city about an hour and half away. And to get to that city we had to go through so many checkpoints and through rebel-held areas. In one area, if they knew someone was a Christian they would capture them and slaughter them on the spot. So I decided not to go. I thought it's not worth it – I'm not going to risk my life. I would just stay with my wife and we would stay in Damascus.

I remember my dad, that week, woke us up in the morning. My dad would spend time with the Lord in the morning every day and one morning that week dad woke us up and said "Let's go." So around 7am we got in the car – dad and mum in the front seat, me and my wife in the back – and we started to drive. I started praying because this is a war zone and I began to pray through that location. As we exited Damascus and headed out on the highway we got to the first checkpoint still early in the morning. We slowed down, with a line of cars behind us. When it was my dad's turn, he opened the window and there were soldiers, guns, tanks, and everyone was ready to fire. The soldier pointed his AK47 at my dad's face while asking for ID. My heart was sinking at this point, my mouth was dry and they were collecting the ID and my dad looked at the soldier in his eyes, still with the machine gun in his face he said "I want to share with you the best gift the world has ever known."

And when I heard him say that as I'm trying to pass him our ID's, my heart just sunk. I thought "This is it, we are going to die'. My dad began to share the gospel with this soldier right there at the checkpoint. You could see that when my dad said I'm going to share the best gift this world has ever known, there was like a blank look on his face – "What are you talking about?" As Dad began to share the gospel with him, I began to notice him lean towards my mum. There was a bag next to him and in the bag, there were Bibles. If I had known that my dad had Bibles in the car, I would never have got in. He began to hand him a Bible and the soldier grabbed it, and my dad was still holding the Bible. The soldier wanted the Bible and was trying to take it, but my dad wouldn't let go of it and in my mind I'm saying "Let go of the Bible, he wants the Bible – just let go of it and let's move on." My dad would not let go of the Bible until he made the soldier promise to read the word of God. He promised and then the soldier opened Dad's door and made him get out of the car. And then he made him pray for him and for all the men at that checkpoint. So, my dad starts praying for all those soldiers.

We jump back in the car and start driving to the next checkpoint. I start praying for my dad and I pray, "Please don't let my dad open his mouth at the next checkpoint please let him stay quiet." We get to the next checkpoint and as we get to the next checkpoint the same thing happens. We slow down and as soon as he opens the window, he says, "I want to share with you the best gift the world has ever known." From checkpoint to checkpoint, checkpoint to checkpoint and at every checkpoint I had the same prayer fearing that at one of those checkpoints there would be radicals who would kill us. And at every checkpoint the first thing my dad would share was about the best gift the world has ever known.

We get to the building where we need to get the document and we stand in line. My dad had that bag of Bibles with him. I stand behind him and it's a crowded building and glass windows – everyone can see and hear. It's our turn, and my dad stepped forward and I stayed back. I thought well, I knew what he was going to do, I knew he was going to share the gospel, and I thought that if I stayed back then if he shared the gospel and got into trouble, then I could take the document and act like I'm not with him and just do it myself. My dad goes forward, and I look to the side and of course my dad begins to share about the best gift the world has ever known. I look to the side and begin to see, and it took some time, but I begin to see tears falling from the women's eyes. And in that moment, it hit me that the people, no matter who they are, are thirsty for truth. And that realisation has changed my life. The reality is there is a thirst for truth they have, and we have the truth for them, we have the gospel for them.

Another aspect of that story, I always challenge people: what are you doing? What are you doing with the best gift the world has ever known? What are you doing with the truth? There is a reality where I feel that the world around us here or wherever we live in the West is thirsty and in need of truth. And we have truth for them. And what are we doing with it? I use myself as an example, to be the weak person thinking about the document, thinking about logic, thinking about what we should say and what we should not say. And thinking about my father, and his zeal for Christ, his heart for Scripture; he has fear but when it comes to the word of God, he has no fear. And then he begins to share the gospel and I just encourage people in that way, to learn the lesson, to be like my dad. People are interested and want to hear and want to share the truth that we have in His name."

There are a few things I observe as I listen to my friends. I hear a spiritual hunger and a consistent and sustained openness to the gospel among the general population. I detect a higher frequency of the miraculous. God's people seem to be more passionately engaged in the purposes of God.

It's true many people in the majority-world do indeed live with hardships such as famine. What is just as real, yet not so visible, is that vast numbers of people living in the West now have a famine living in them. I hope we are at the tide's lowest ebb in the West and that the gospel tide may start to flow in.

Does this whet your appetite? I hope so.

I want the tide to come in in the westernised world. When I talk to my friends in some of the areas where God is strongly at work, I want us to have similar stories to exchange of all God is doing across the nations. Imagine a time when the day of rock pools is eclipsed by such a tidal surge of the life of God that it would not be able to be measured in a rock pool way anymore. At such a time even the contours and shape of the coastline are reshaped.

2
A TURNING TIDE
TIME FOR THE TIDE TO TURN

Throughout Scripture, it is not uncommon to see times when the tide of God's activity amongst His people seemed to be at a low ebb and by contrast times when great moves of His Spirit are in evidence. We see this same ebbing and flowing throughout church history. I remain persuaded that there are promises in Scripture that assure us of a global incoming tide that shall be experienced before the return of Christ.

> *It shall come to pass in the latter days that the mountain of the house of the LORD shall be established as the highest of the mountains, and shall be lifted up above the hills; and all the nations shall flow to it, and many peoples shall come, and say: 'Come let us go up to the mountain of the LORD, to the house of the God of Jacob,*

> *that he may teach us his ways and that we may walk in*
> *his paths.*

ISAIAH 2:2-3 (ESV)

Visible, prominent, dominating the horizon, unable to be hid, attractive and pulsating with life, drawing people to Christ!

That's a great future and that gives us hope. But we also have much to learn from those who lived during the low points. Nehemiah was one who lived during a very low-tide moment for God's people. He could only see the remnants of the walls of Jerusalem and so he mourned. I mourn. He lamented. I lament. Humility, for those of us who identify with the tide being out, is an appropriate heart posture. Yet what we see in other areas of the world does not allow our hope to be snuffed out. I rejoice at all I see and hear of elsewhere. It gives me hope that God can do it again in my land, area, town and yours too. As I read church history I see that often at times of low ebb God comes afresh. May it be so.

I used to think that lamenting showed a lack of faith. But I've since learned the difference between lament and despair. To despair is to have no hope, because the situation really is

16

hopeless! But that's not what lament is. Lamenting is reflecting on what you know to be less than God's design and purpose for something and acknowledging that the present reality is not as God intended. It is seeing things as they really are and grieving all the ways it falls short of what God says.

Nehemiah felt deeply how God felt about the state of His people and His purposes and it moved him to do something about it. To have the privilege of God sharing the feelings of His heart with us finds us often feeling quite weighty emotions. We enter into partnership with Him on His mission not simply as emotionless, robotic servants but in relationship with Him, feeling what He feels, walking through it alongside Him.

These are not days to lament and not act, they are days to lament, humble ourselves, wait on God in prayer and then begin to arise as God comes with His empowering presence breathing fresh life into His church. Receptivity to the gospel, born of the Holy Spirit, will once again pervade the atmosphere. The soil of people's hearts is already being turned into fertile ground for the gospel to land.

God is in the long process of changing a culture and seeing His kingdom grow but He seems to have a strong preference for starting fresh moves in very small ways. For example Gideon was the last and least and David was the youngest of all Jesse's sons. There is the city of Jerusalem, but He chose small villages like Bethlehem and Nazareth for His Son to be born and grow up in. And Jesus told stories of lost sheep, elderly widows, and mustard-seed-like faith. Small beginnings yet full of kingdom hope.

We need to harness these two dynamics of hope and lament to help move us into fruitful action. Reasons to lament might be easier to see, so let's consider some reasons to hope that the tide may turn.

GLOBAL CHANGES ARE UNDERWAY

For my generation, the one born post-World War Two, we have largely been shielded from the adversity that most of the world throughout most of history has had to endure. We've mostly been spared from wars, economic collapse, pandemics and natural disasters. Instead, we have lived through an age that has seen such great strides in healthcare and medicine that many westerners even view death as something that can be managed and pushed back ever further. Maybe it will even, one day, become an inconvenience that will largely be eradicated. Yet despite, or perhaps because of, this unprecedented prosperity the western world has become faithless.

So how might God begin to turn the tide in places where the spiritual temperature is currently low? What kinds of things might He employ to begin to change such a barren spiritual landscape?

GLOBAL SHAKINGS

At the time of writing the world has been shaken by the COVID-19 pandemic. When I began writing this book, I thought perhaps only making a small reference to it thinking it might not be such a dominant thing. I have changed my mind.

In 1918, hard on the heels of the First World War, the world was struck by what came to be known as the Spanish flu. "Lasting from February 1918 to April 1920, it infected 500 million people – about a third of the world's population at the time – in four successive waves. The death toll is typically estimated to have been somewhere between 20 million and 50 million, although estimates range from a conservative 17 million to a possible high of 100 million, making it one of the deadliest pandemics in human history."[5]

I have witnessed how this current pandemic is shaking people so that they consider their frailty, the uncertainty of life and the foolishness of putting hope in 'things'. The sudden vulnerability of the world to catastrophe can make hearts ask questions.

I'm hoping history will repeat itself. My home town of Lowestoft experienced the last mainland revival in England in 1921.

A typical account from the early days in Lowestoft read like this:

> *I shall never forget that night as long as I live... As I entered the church again and stood looking at the people, brother Edwards paused for a moment and asked if there were any others coming to the inquiry room. We had been*

---

[5] en.wikipedia.org/wiki/Spanish_flu

praying for "showers" that night and he gave us a "cloud burst".

They came from all parts of the building and filled the deacons' vestry. It was just like waiting [in a long queue] outside some theatre... I went to Douglas Brown and said "what are we to do?", "You cannot deal with all these people one by one!"

So we just opened the school room, and in they came – 50 -60 people to start with... I had been speaking for only a few minutes, and then the door opened and another batch came in, and all was confusion for a few minutes. Then I tried to speak to them again; and again the door opened, and another batch came in. It was a wonderful sight.[6]

The revival that started in Lowestoft spread to other parts of East Anglia. Scotland was also affected through the witness of the fishing community who followed the seasonal migration of herring along the east coast. Those used to light revival fires in these places found themselves also involved in similar spreading of the 'fire of revival' in Ulster.

---

[6] Rev Hugh P E Ferguson, *The Keswick Week*, 1921, p. 240.

Might it be that even through the horrors of this current pandemic that God is opening the hearts of people to thirst, look, ask about Him? That He has it in His heart's plan to bring many to Christ in and through all we are experiencing? The tide can come in on the back of a storm.

ECONOMIC CHANGE

Great turmoil in global markets is something we've had to deal with several times. The days we live in will be no different. We simply cannot expect what many of us have lived in to be how things will be forever. All things will be shaken and only that which is built on Christ will stand. It is quite possible that a shift in the balance of economic centres will take place in the coming years and a move from West to East will have a huge economic impact.

MASS MIGRATION

The early years of the 21st century have brought unprecedented mass migration and a huge displacement of tens of millions of people. Many left their homes and lands with nothing but what they were wearing. One of the major destination points for these migrants and refugees are the rich, safe western nations of Europe and North America. Might it be that amongst those crossing over the Mediterranean Sea in small dinghies are those who will emerge as major leaders in churches in the West? We must be ready and humble to be led by those God brings from such places of great upheaval.

A few years ago, I was at a global leaders' conference in the Middle East. Whilst there I felt God speak to me about an earthquake but not of land, when tectonic plates shift, but an earthquake of people. Large numbers being displaced and violently moved across the nations. I held on to this word for about three days as it didn't quite seem to fit. On the penultimate day, during a prayer time, I felt this was the right time to share. As I stood and spoke, the hotel we were in experienced a small but noticeable earthquake. I think my prophetic word did not need much weighing that day! It was almost like God underlining it with a red marker pen – "I'm serious about this!"

Paul had a vision[7] of a man from Macedonia beckoning to him; well, if you are in areas of the world where the tide is in and the gospel is flourishing, may I add my voice to you: please come over and help the many of us for whom the tide is out. You have wisdom, experience, insight on things God has taught you on being effective witnesses for Christ. You've seen many come to faith and many churches planted and whole communities impacted, you are welcome to come.

God is building one new humanity in Christ[8] on Earth made up of every ethnic group, language, culture, tribe and people, and we each need each other. These are the days when the powerful church of the majority-world can come to the aid of the westernised world who in many cases first brought the gospel to those nations. What a chance to pay back with interest the investment of the gospel!

---

[7] Acts 16:6-10.
[8] Ephesians 2:15.

GLOBAL PARTNERSHIPS

It is not just those displaced through persecution or war or natural disaster who will find their way into the westernised world. God has friendships He is establishing, as leaders of movements and families of churches find a heart connection with others sometimes many thousands of miles away. These partnerships for the gospel will bring blessing to both. This is an emerging trend, happening right now, on a scale that has never been seen before.

These new partnerships are being powered by the internet and (pandemic aside) the ease of global travel. God used the Roman road system, in the days of the early church, to facilitate the spread of the gospel, and in our day it is Wi-Fi and aeroplanes having a similar multiplying effect. The advent of high speed internet connection means I can find myself in video calls with people from many nations in the course of a single day. Whilst such calls are not a replacement for the unique place of meeting face to face, they are, I believe, a provision of God intended for the global advance of the gospel.

Learning, equipping and partnering across the globe, born out of deep friendships and birthed in the purposes of God, are happening like never before. These friendships are giving rise to collaborations across nations with ever increasing influence and fruitfulness. We are seeing the emergence of a true global church with a global theology and a global mission.

CHURCH, SEIZE THE DAY!

For many people the ability to gather for corporate worship in the way and with the ease of past years has been badly affected by the COVID-19 pandemic. Huge waves of infection control saw large numbers of churches switching incredibly quickly to online versions of their services. Innovation and technological skills had to be sourced almost overnight. What extraordinary days.

I am convinced that the public physical gathering of the local church is a vital part of its corporate life and is not lost for good, as some have said in the pandemic. Yet there are new and as yet unexplored paths of reaching people that now present themselves.

In the first seven chapters of the book of Acts the church had been gathering in large numbers visibly and effectively. In Acts 8, after Stephen is stoned to death and persecution breaks out, the church is scattered and forced underground. Even in this apparently hostile environment, the church flourished.

Some ten years later, in Acts 11, we read of the emergence of a move of God in Antioch. It was a place no one expected, amongst people not targeted, through a group of people not sent and at a time not planned!

Sometimes what God is working on can take time to work out but it always does come through. We must see whatever circumstances we are in not as the end of the church's fruitfulness but as fresh doors of opportunity for the gospel to thrive.

A NEW CULTURE OF 'EVERYONE A WITNESS'

As terrible as COVID-19 is, a far more deadly thing resides amongst us day after day – the death and sin that plagues humanity is something we live with every day of our lives, and we've been aware of it since we became followers of Christ, yet

27

we live with perhaps less urgency about this plague, which kills 100% of people. A good doctor will tell their patient what is wrong with them and what can be done about it, even if the truth is a bit scary. I don't want a doctor who tells me "Everything will be fine" and doesn't tell me about the treatment that will save my life.

We have been lulled into apathy and indifference. We've been distracted and preoccupied by other less important matters. We've been intimidated into silence; fearful of those who do not believe such a plague exists. When it had to, the church made the pivot online in the storm of COVID-19. Now we need another massive pivot moment, this time not 'every church online' but 'everyone a witness'.

I believe there is a growing longing in the hearts of God's people who live where the tide is out. A growing ache for a fresh visitation of God. Will such longings translate themselves into prayers and ultimately fresh choices of what we give our lives to?

As God, by His Spirit, begins to change the culture amongst His people, it prepares us for fresh impact. In recent years, within the family of churches I help lead, we have been investing in large-scale corporate prayer. I am convinced, from both scriptural principles and church history, that engaging large numbers of God's people in this activity is of strategic importance ahead of a move of God. After investing in this for some years we are now beginning to focus on another major cultural change required: to see everyone a witness for Christ. Prayer and sharing the gospel go together and form two of the major basic foundations of being a disciple of Christ.

The reason for this book is to hopefully inspire you to embrace the journey of becoming a witness for Christ so that over time we see 'everyone a witness' forming as a culture and a way of life. I find my own sense of smallness and helplessness is often diluted in a corporate prayer meeting where I feel I am amongst people doing business with God. I find the same thing is true when I become aware that I am part of a whole community of people ready, willing, equipped and active in being witnesses for Christ throughout daily life. Large numbers of even small creatures can have huge effects. Just ask anyone who has ever seen a swarm of locusts!

I don't think the next incoming tide will be as a result of an initiative or because of a few mightily gifted people but instead because of an army of thousands of ordinary believers who have become witnesses. What if, in our church gatherings, we regularly heard stories from across the church of how, in daily life, God was touching people's lives and people were finding Christ or moving towards knowing Him? What if we regularly had space in our meetings for people who have come to Christ to give their stories of how it happened? These two things would feed and nurture a culture of 'everyone a witness' more and more. If we add this to a growing culture of the 'prayers of many', wow… Come on church, let's seize the moment!

WHAT ABOUT YOU? ARE YOU IN?

Your people will offer themselves freely on the day of your power, in holy garments; from the womb of the morning, the dew of your youth will be yours.

PSALM 110:3 (ESV)

When the tide comes in it is because God has done it. But He looks for His people to be the agents of His purposes, both through bringing this new move of God to birth in prayer and then by serving the incoming tide through obedient witness.

And we will see Him bringing people to Christ and planting and strengthening churches to the ends of the Earth.

I'm inviting you into a journey of culture change. If the tide is going to turn it requires a willing and obedient people through which He can work. For those of us living in nations where the tide of gospel fruitfulness is presently out; this is not the time to just lament. These are days to give ourselves afresh to the Lord with unswerving obedience and commit to doing what He shows us. Let us live not for ourselves or for a comfortable way of life.

This is the call to 'everyone a witness'. This is the call to trust Him with our lives and surrender to Him the genuine troubles and distresses that living in this world brings, knowing He is able and willing to take care of all these things for us. We may well have to learn how to thrive in adversity, as most people who follow Christ in the global church already do. Are you willing to learn some new things, to take some steps into the unknown, to press to the edges of your current experience and get some new stories to share?

There is nothing so motivating as a large number of people in a shared endeavour for God and when stories start to filter through amongst the ranks of believers it really encourages us all to press on. One person's success and breakthrough is everyone's. Are you willing to actively be a witness for Christ? Are you willing to live sold out for Him and His purposes?

It is a most glorious and unusual life, filled with great cost and at times pain and set back. But it is why we are alive: to join wholeheartedly in His great commission to "go and make disciples of all nations"[9], knowing He is with us, empowering us by His Holy Spirit to be His witnesses to the very end of the age. Let us see 'everyone a witness' and the tide of many people coming to faith in Christ coming in. Let the adventure begin; are you in?

1. O soul, are you weary and troubled?
No light in the darkness you see?
There's light for a look at the Saviour,
And life more abundant and free!

---

[9] Matthew 28:19.

Refrain:
Turn your eyes upon Jesus,
Look full in His wonderful face,
And the things of Earth will grow strangely dim,
In the light of His glory and grace.

2. Through death into life everlasting
He passed, and we follow Him there;
O'er us sin no more hath dominion—
For more than conqu'rors we are!

3. His Word shall not fail you—He promised;
Believe Him, and all will be well:
Then go to a world that is dying,
His perfect salvation to tell!

HELEN LEMMELL
PUBLIC DOMAIN, 1922

3
A UKRAINIAN
POWER CUT
BEING READY AND EMPOWERED

For a number of years I served churches across Russia and Ukraine, helping establish training centres for church leaders. One Sunday, I was preaching to a fairly large congregation in a largely mining area of south-east Ukraine. Many hundreds were gathered in a former Communist Party building. The large auditorium felt quite imposing with the tiered seating stretching back high above my eyeline.

My sermon was prepared and the time came to speak. As I stepped forward a power cut pitched the entire hall into darkness. We had no power, no lights and no sound. I was taken aback but no one else was. Power cuts at that time were just a part of the normal rhythm of life and sure enough after 10-15 minutes all was restored and I was able to carry on.

Let's analyse all the different elements that enabled that sermon to take place. I needed proximity to people to give the message, a willingness to be there, to move from my comfort zone and feel vulnerable. I needed content, so I had to be prepared and have a readiness to share. What also became very obvious was that I also needed an external power source to help me effectively convey the message to my hearers. This combination of proximity, readiness, a message and the power to convey it is at the heart of seeing 'everyone a witness'.

A LIVING EXAMPLE

The believers in Ukraine are remarkable examples of how to thrive in adversity. Not only have they faced many years of hostility to the gospel in the recent communist past, but they now face many economic, social and political challenges. The way they did life was itself a gospel message to the community around. They served the very poorest and marginalised in their communities with a robust intentional vision orientated around sharing the gospel.

In one large congregation the earnestness and passion of the corporate worship in sub-zero temperatures, in yet another stark former Communist Party building, was quite something! At the start of the service a lady, not a member of the church, and as far as I know not a believer, brought her son into the meeting. The young lad could only have been about four years old. His pale complexion revealed more than just cold to be the issue. My interpreter informed me that he had a form of blood cancer with a poor prognosis for the future. His mother knew that the church prayed for people and had seen many healed. She had walked in off the street to ask the church to pray for him. The volume and intensity of prayer around the room reverberated long and loud. Sadly, I do not know the outcome. What I do know is that the church had placed itself in proximity to the people, and had a message and a readiness to engage that resulted in the community knowing they could come with their needs to the church. What the church also evidently displayed was that they had power to convey and demonstrate that message.

What if your local church developed a similar reputation as this church had? What if people turned up on a Sunday or at other gatherings bringing the sick, the needy and the desperate knowing you were full of love and full of power? It reminds me of the early days of Acts when the church was known to meet in Solomon's Colonnade, a place well known to the community in Jerusalem. People came with their needs and many were saved simply by being in proximity to this 'Jesus community'.

A GROWING CONTEXT FOR THE GOSPEL TO FLOURISH

I have often found extreme need heightens receptivity to the gospel. People just start to ask questions and they go looking for answers when they find themselves faced with circumstances they cannot solve. It is, I believe, one of the reasons why churches in nations facing economic, social or political upheaval often grow with vigour. As the reality of human frailty dawns on large numbers of people, they feel the need to search for answers. Need brings them to their senses like it did for the prodigal son in Luke 15.

As I write, the world is in the grip of the COVID-19 pandemic. Once secure and wealthy nations find themselves in uncharted waters as their economies are stretched in ways unimaginable. Healthcare systems are stretched to breaking point. Such upheavals shake people out of apathy and indifference to God.

I was at a funeral recently and a lady I know who is not a believer said to me, "You're a religious man aren't you? I think this pandemic is the will of God, what do you think?" I would say such a proactive approach has not been common in my experience.

In answer to her question, I don't think God has visited a pandemic on the Earth to punish or judge. I think all sorts of earthly dysfunctions, famines, earthquakes and disasters show the truth: that Earth is in bondage to decay. I also think that God works through the mess we have made of things. Even through the consequences of The Fall, God is able to bring about His purposes, which are the saving of many souls and the destroying of the works of the evil one. I left my questioner with the thought that in it all, Jesus still loves us.

So how can we ensure we are prepared and empowered to be witnesses with power?

ALWAYS BE READY

But in your hearts honour Christ the Lord as holy, always being prepared to make a defence to anyone who asks you for a reason for the hope that is in you; yet do it with gentleness and respect...

1 PETER 3:15 (ESV)

I recall one day walking past the Natural History Museum in London and being stopped by a man with bulging eyeballs, a red face and the veins on his neck pumping with zeal. He asked me if I knew Christ. I explained I did. He then asked me if I had shared my faith that day. I answered that so far I had not but was ready when opportunity arose. He retorted, becoming ever more red in the face and the eyeballs bulging even more, that this simply was not good enough. I "MUST" share my faith each day.

I reflected later on this incident. What stood out, apart from the veins in his neck, was that he was not an embodiment of good news. He was a stress machine wanting to put a heavy yoke on me. This was not the partnering with Christ spoken of in Scripture but instead was man's effort that did not look like "good news to all mankind"[10] at all. His was an attempt to place a legalistic burden on me.

What I am advocating is learning how to "always be ready"[11], anticipating and being proactive (probably more than we have been), but led in partnership with the Holy Spirit, where we can witness freely rather than being driven by human effort. Some would argue with me that we must witness to anyone and everyone, anywhere and anytime. I understand that challenge and no less a person than C.H.Spurgeon made it:[12]

If in your street, a man shall perish through not knowing the Saviour, and you never made an effort to instruct him, how will you be guiltless at the last great day?

There is an important balance between being ready, willing and desiring to share, and feeling that someone's eternal destiny rests on our shoulders. But there is a difference too

---

[10] Mark 16:15.

[11] 1 Peter 3:15.

[12] Tweet by @SpurgeonMBTS: 9.30pm, 19th August 2020. www.twitter.com/SpurgeonMBTS/status/1296182817232236548

between passive staying and active going! We are to be neither passive nor driven.

I do not dispute that many have the grace to take this proactive lifestyle, I applaud them and actually stand in awe of them often, but even they do not find all their conversations lead to people coming to Christ. Something more than human effort is required.

An old man I knew, who was not a believer, was close to death. We had become good friends and had enjoyed many conversations over the years including discussing the gospel. So I visited him wanting one last chance to see if there was any openness to Jesus. He raised the subject of spiritual matters and said to me, "I don't understand how someone as intelligent as you can believe such utter rubbish!" I tried my best but in the end was not able to make much observable progress. He died a short while after. I do not live without hope though. Even the hardest heart, in the last hours of life, can make eternal transactions. When all the arguments and pretence is removed and a man is left staring into eternity with nothing left to cling to, many prayers are then prayed. I am sure we will get surprises in heaven.

LED BY THE SPIRIT

The Spirit told Philip, "Go to that chariot and stay near it."

ACTS 8:29 (NIV)

The Holy Spirit does seem to lead us to certain people at certain times: what some call divine appointments. In the above verse, Philip is directed where to go so that he can speak to the Ethiopian man in the chariot. Sarah from Canterbury shared with me one such 'appointment' she had.

I'd been praying for opportunities in lockdown and praying about how we can go across those boundaries to people who I wouldn't naturally mix with and just stepping through that fear of people I might find a bit intimidating. I had to go for some tests at the hospital and the oncology ward is a super depressing waiting room. It was really packed with people that day and the staff was running around 40 minutes late. There was a lady who was just, well, very different to me, but she was clearly agitated. She seemed aggressive and was stomping around the waiting room, swearing at the nurses and you could tell she was really agitated. She looked like she might explode. Well, that's the sort of 'Holy Spirit highlighting' that you need isn't it? Here's someone feeling distressed and clearly in need. Then she came and sat next to me. To be honest, I was feeling a little bit scared by her but I was like "Ok thank you Jesus, this is the answer to my prayer – the opportunity to chat to somebody who would normally scare me a little bit."

I began to ask her some questions about how she was doing, and just chatted with her. She instantly opened up about all this horrendous stuff that had been going on in her life quite loudly in a very quiet waiting room. So I was having to fight back my embarrassment. Bless her, she was sharing all this horrible stuff and clearly quite angry because this was the last straw having to wait an extra 40 minutes for this potentially life changing news. I didn't even say anything particularly profound, but I said "Do you know what? I'm a Christian actually and I'd just love to pray for you." And she was like "Oh yes please!!" So again I was like "It's a really busy waiting room and everyone is listening…". But I said to myself "just go for it". So I just prayed for the incredible love of Jesus to meet with her and for her to know her true value in Him, for the presence and peace of God that is just supernatural and beyond understanding to surround her. As I was praying it was just incredible. It was like the presence of God just drew really close and her whole body relaxed. She had a mask on but you could tell she was

smiling behind the mask and just her whole demeanour
changed as I was praying for the destiny of Jesus over her
– His peace met with her in an incredible way.

The Holy Spirit does also seem to give individuals a bias or sense of being drawn to particular types and groups of people. You might find certain kinds of people drop into your mind even as you read this; the poor, business leaders, the elderly, children, refugees etc. These leanings should be taken note of – they are often an indication of a call from God to those people. Peter was called to the Jews and Paul to the Gentiles. They could articulate this quite clearly and confidently.

The above being said, we are all to have a mindset of on-going readiness to witness for Christ to anyone at any time in any place in any way that is helpful. Avoiding the extremities of being driven by legalistic duty or rendered ineffective through apathy and inaction.

But to live this way might need something of a culture shift. We need to train ourselves so that we are predisposed to think and behave instinctively, intuitively and habitually in a certain way. An adjusting of how we live, what we value and prioritise in life. These changes to our personal and church cultures require several components.

In the West we are not so used to people being hungry to know Christ. We are more used to pushback, scepticism or even incredulity. As a result many Christians have reconditioned themselves, heads down, mouths shut. But what happens when more people are asking and searching and increasing numbers of people actually *do* want to know what the gospel is? My contention is that just maybe in these days we should be more ready than we have been at any point in our lives.

I love fly fishing for trout. I can tell when I go whether the conditions are favourable or not. Some days, with a ripple on the water, not too hot and a bit of cloud cover, you can almost guarantee a fish on every cast. On other sunny, hot, still, clear water days, just go home or sunbathe! My hunch is the conditions are becoming favourable for a very fruitful season of 'everyone a witness'.

But the readiness I am speaking about is not just about speaking words but about demonstrating the heart of God.

So then, as we have opportunity, let us do good to everyone, and especially to those who are of the household of faith.

GALATIANS 6:10 (ESV)

This can be empowerment of the poor or praying for those who are unwell, or meeting all kinds of needs – 'doing good' in the community. It is all a vital part of witnessing.

But as for you, continue in what you have learned and have firmly believed, knowing from whom you learned it.

2 TIMOTHY 3:14 (ESV)

It is not just what we say but the integrity and quality of our lives backing up the message that validates it. We must never think demonstrating the heart of God in kindness and serving is somehow less than witnessing. It adds credibility when we do get to actually speak of the Saviour and what He has done in our lives. People watch more than they listen in these days where the internet has multiplied so many voices into our world.

NOT ASHAMED

> *For I am not ashamed of the gospel, for it is the power of God for salvation to everyone who believes, to the Jew first and also to the Greek.*
>
> ROMANS 1:16 (ESV)

> *... do not be ashamed of the testimony about our Lord*
>
> 2 TIMOTHY 1:8 (ESV)

> *... which is why I suffer as I do. But I am not ashamed, for I know whom I have believed, and I am convinced that he is able to guard until that day what has been entrusted to me*
>
> 2 TIMOTHY 1:12 (ESV)

The above verses and others in Scripture alert us to an internal barrier to being witnesses for Christ: that of shame. The fear of being laughed at, ridiculed, offending people, self-consciousness, feeling "It is not my place to speak, no one will want to hear what I have to say". All of these things can press in on us with great weight.

Knowing we are a minority – often laughed at, ridiculed, not taken seriously – does affect our confidence. It is also of note that western liberal society is ever more hostile to traditional orthodox biblical Christian teaching that may challenge the way we live. No one wants to lose friends or be isolated in the workplace. Sometimes we feel the hostility of society and it is all too easy to keep quiet or simply freeze in certain settings. The devil wants to place a gagging order on each of us. He likes nothing better than to intimidate us, accuse us, whisper lies to us. Anything to stop us praying and stop us witnessing for Christ.

We need to liberate our tongues and more importantly our fears. Paul writes urging believers not to be ashamed. I feel the challenge of his words.

YOU WILL RECEIVE POWER

But you will receive power when the Holy Spirit has come upon you, and you will be my witnesses in Jerusalem and in all Judea and Samaria, and to the end of the earth.

ACTS 1:8 (ESV)

After I received Christ into my life, I struggled for some months wondering, "Am I really saved?", "Did I do it right?", "Why don't I feel different?" Two things happened to me that

48

changed that: one gradual, one immediate. The gradual change was that, as I became more and more acquainted with the Bible and promises of God, I learned to define my reality from what the Bible said was true of me rather than letting my feelings determine my perspective. The second was an unexpected and life-affecting visitation of the Holy Spirit, which I later learned was referred to by many as "the Baptism of the Holy Spirit". I had been saved, the Holy Spirit was indwelling from my conversion, but this second experience of the Holy Spirit was an infilling, a flooding, a game changer, an immediate empowerment and perspective changer. I 'felt' the assurance of being saved. I felt the Fatherhood and nearness of God. I also found myself wanting to see the gospel come to many more people and, together with friends in church, we thought and dreamed incessantly of how we might witness Christ to the people in the town I lived in.

The book of Acts says the infilling of the Holy Spirit is intended to be the catalyst for us all being effective witnesses for Christ. Some may argue with my theology of a second or subsequent experience, but whatever your view on that, the same Holy Spirit empowerment is surely beyond dispute. The intention of God's heart is to see 'everyone a witness' achieved by an empowering of the Holy Spirit. This is an ongoing desire of God and how we need a fresh infilling today especially in the West!

YOU WILL BE GIVEN THE WORDS

And when they bring you before the synagogues and the rulers and the authorities, do not be anxious about how you should defend yourself or what you should say, for the Holy Spirit will teach you in that very hour what you ought to say.

LUKE 12:11-12 (ESV)

In over 40 years now as a follower of Christ, I have heard much teaching and seen many courses, techniques, plans, systems for being effective witnesses. If I started to list it all here, it probably would fill another chapter! Many of the people, teaching, courses, techniques and methods I have learned from have been such a help to me and many others. I am all for being equipped with tools to use, as sometimes having a simple framework to follow can really help our confidence in witnessing for Christ.

Having said all of that, I do think the emphasis of the verses is not that our confidence should rest on our preparation. Instead, even when we might bring lots of hard work, study and skill into the context, nevertheless we can rely on the Holy Spirit to nudge us with the right things to say in the moment. Power comes by the activity of the Holy Spirit working with, but also beyond, our preparation and ability. Salvation does belong to the Lord. The Holy Spirit can take the smallest, simplest of things we share, things that sometimes just drop into our minds to say and, like a small seed planted in good soil, life springs forth.

4
A RUSSIAN
RAILWAY STATION
LEARNING TO COMMUNICATE THE GOSPEL

"It can't be that difficult" I thought to myself as I entered the Moscow central railway station en route to one of the international airports for my flight home. What I had not anticipated was that all the signs would only be in Russian. The Cyrillic alphabet bears little resemblance to the Latin one. There weren't even those little plane icons indicating which platform the airport shuttle went from. Worse still, there are two Moscow international airports served by this train station. I needed to get on the right train to the right airport. No one I asked spoke any English whatsoever and my limited Russian was a combination of simple pleasantries and complex theological words I had picked up during the training sessions I had been attending. What I did not know was the word for airport or even how to spell the airport in question!

In desperation I resorted to outstretched arms and aeroplane noises interspersed with the name of the airport I wanted. Most people just watched me but eventually a kind soul pointed, nodded and smiled. It was the right one. The relief I felt as I arrived at the right airport is still with me!

It's hard to get to where you want to go if you can't communicate. If we want to be faithful and fruitful witnesses we need to know how to communicate the gospel simply yet sufficiently; to convey its essential truth and the heart of God behind it. Preferably without waving your arms and making aeroplane noises.

WHAT TO COMMUNICATE

In order to be fluent when it comes to talking about the gospel, it helps to know the bigger story of God's mission. It helps to see that each of us are part of a huge global family, part of God's unfolding purposes on Earth. Rightly understood, this gives us a sense of meaning, purpose, belonging and perspective on our lives. We are not insignificant even though we are small. We are part of something global and eternal. We fit in history as part of something much bigger than ourselves.

Yet there is also a very tender personal and intimate aspect to the gospel. Like the love story in the Song of Solomon, each of us is individually the object of God's extraordinary and personal affection. Helping people who come to Christ see both these aspects of salvation, in my view, aids future maturity in God. We receive salvation as individuals but we are saved into a people and a family.

The gospel, at heart, is simple, and simple to convey. Seeing the church embrace a culture of 'everyone a witness' depends on us grasping that simplicity. It means that whether child or adult, educated or not, rich or poor, no one is beyond the impact of the life-changing message we have been entrusted with.

Paul reflecting on the essence of 'everyone a witness' said,

For I delivered to you as of first importance what I also received: that Christ died for our sins in accordance with the Scriptures, that he was buried, that he was raised on the third day in accordance with the Scriptures.

1 CORINTHIANS 15:3-4 (ESV)

This is the gospel. There is more but never less to say. It really can help us to practice simple ways of communicating the essential truth of the gospel.

Paul, in referring to the thing that is of "first importance", is making the point that our communicating of the gospel and witnessing to the reality of the work of Christ is the key thing for the church to do collectively and individually. There are no precise scripted words. My attempt to sum it up goes like this:

God created the world. He made it good and perfect; everything functioned well. He created human beings, male and female, in His image. We enjoyed the blessings of the wonderful relationship we had with God and with the magnificent world God had made for us to enjoy. He entrusted us with looking after the world – partnering with Him in spreading His glory and fruitfulness all over the planet.

Sadly, Adam and Eve believed they could live life without the need for God. They came to feel they wanted to live independently from God. No need to be accountable to God; instead choosing to live for themselves, answerable to no one. They thought they could do life just fine without God.

Their choices opened the door to all manner of sin and inevitably to death spreading throughout mankind and to a breaking away from the God who made and sustained them. The Earth itself felt the reverberations of this terrible decision. Nothing now worked the way it should and life became hard and brutal with much suffering and sorrow. Even in the midst of the stunning beauty of all God had made, something now was fundamentally wrong and dysfunctional. What a fall!

Distanced from God, our nature became governed by sinful desires and evil. We found ourselves without God and without hope or certainty in a world now broken. And we have lived in this broken condition ever since. People from one generation to the next wonder why they are here? What is the purpose of life? Is there more to everything than just living and then dying?

Many try to fix the brokenness of the world through human advancement, education, science, economic or political strategies. Others look for answers in money, pleasure, relationships, travel, achievement... But all these things just leave us with an aching heart longing for fulfilment. Still others block out the sounds of such big questions and live for the moment, thinking when they die that is it.

Unaware, we face an eternity of separation from God as a consequence of our rebellion and guilt before God. This experience and place the Bible calls and describes as 'hell', something and somewhere we need to be saved from, but cannot do that with our own efforts. Instead, we need a saviour.

Into this sorry and critical situation the Bible (in John 3:16) tells us God took action: *"For God so loved the world, he gave his only son that whoever believes in him should not perish but have everlasting life'*. God the Father took action to save us, motivated by pure love, in spite of our wandering from Him, He pursued us.

Jesus, the son of God, became a man, a second Adam if you like, but also unlike Adam. Jesus' work was to make it possible for every person to have this relationship with God restored. He could not have done this just as a man or He Himself would have been sinful. But because He was also fully God and therefore without sin, He could break the curse of the fall mankind had brought about. He lived a sinless life, obedient to all God, His Father, asked of Him, even death on a cross.

His sacrifice was sufficient for everyone in the world to be saved from the terrible and inescapable prison of sin and death all mankind was in. This happens as each of us believe that Christ was who He said He was and that His death and resurrection are completely sufficient to save us from our sins. He did all that was required for us to be saved.

By that simple act of faith we are brought to a 'new birth', we are cleansed from all our guilt, sin and shame by His work on the cross. The apostle John tells us that for as many as believed in His name, He gave them the right to be called the children of God[13]. Whoever comes to Christ by faith will be saved. His righteousness is given to us as a free gift. His rising from the dead defeats our great enemy – death, we are given

---

[13] John 1:12.

eternal life and reconnected in relationship to God the Father again.

We may, at times, still sin or not feel much different, but the reality is that a huge change has taken place. Our nature is now alive in Christ and filled with His righteousness. Not only forgiven but holy in God's sight. His Holy Spirit, God Himself, lives within us. We become the dwelling place of God. As God walked with Adam and Eve, He now walks with us.

And then one day Christ will return from heaven and on that day all things will be made anew by God. All the consequences of mankind's fall will be finally and fully removed. Everything God planned when He made the world will be restored, in and through the work of Christ. This is what is of first importance!

COMMUNICATE WITH LOVE

Making the gospel accessible and clear to people is vital, but so is the motivation behind it. Paul reflects in 1 Corinthians 13 that knowledge and spiritual power may be present but love is the key ingredient. 'Everyone a witness' is not some legalistic duty for us all to add onto the Christian life, it is the overspill of love we feel for people. I listen to people I know love me. I take their opinion very seriously. The people that have had the greatest effect on my life have been those I knew loved me.

The ministry of John and Carol Wimber has had huge positive influence upon the church in many parts of the globe. What is less publicly known is the influence a man called Gunner Payne first had on them. Carol writes of Gunner,

> *That man was a Christian, and what he was because of Jesus in him, was the strongest argument for Christianity ever stated. He led hundreds of us to the Lord. One to one. He believed you must win a person to yourself by loving them, before you had the right to tell them what you believe. "First win them to yourself, then introduce them to your lord".[14]*

I think of Peggy Woods, a widow who, when my wife Sue came to know Christ, would invite her and her friend round

---

[14] Carol Wimber, *John Wimber: The Way It Was* (Hodder & Stoughton, 1999), p. 69.

for tea each week. She would do Bible studies with them, pouring out all she knew of Christ into their young lives. She did it out of love for them and for Christ.

If the effect of this book were only to stir thoughts of structural change it would have missed a key goal. We must ask Jesus to baptise us afresh into His love for people. This is a supernatural thing as life often presents pressures that suppress love. The power of the Holy Spirit to anoint us with "the greatest ... love"[15] is to be sought and longed for.

People are looking for authenticity in how someone lives, not just factual correctness in what they say. Information is everywhere, integrity not so much. We don't need any more preachers who have a platform but who don't live the life of Christ. The more we love people as churches and individuals, the more receptive they will be to the gospel message.

---

[15] 1 Corinthians 13:13.

HEARING AND OBSERVING PEOPLE

> *For as I passed along and observed the objects of your worship, I found also an altar with this inscription: "To the unknown god." What therefore you worship as unknown, this I proclaim to you.*

ACTS 17:23 (ESV)

Taking time to observe and listen can help us find where the hunger and thirst in someone is. Paul did this in Athens before he engaged with his hearers.

I was on a flight and a conversation began with the young Dutch girl next to me and another lady next to her. We exchanged pleasantries and each said why they were travelling. The Dutch girl was passionate about tackling climate change and helping save the planet. Once she knew I was a Christian she asked "What do you think Jesus would think of environmental activism?" I could have said, "Let's not bother about that because what you need is a Saviour and He died on the cross for you." Instead, as I listened to the passionate life commitment she had to the environmental cause, I began to talk about God's wonderful creation, man's poor stewardship of the Earth, the preciousness of the Earth to God and His promise of a renewing and merging of the heavens and Earth when Jesus returns, and the heart of God for the poor. Not only did this really open up the conversation with all three of us but I later was able to bring it round to my conviction that the fundamental issue is the sinfulness of humanity and our need for a Saviour. Listening before engaging helped me to speak helpfully.

My Dutch friend was just one example of a wider cultural trend. James Emery White, in his teaching on the "rise of the nones"[16] (those with no religious affiliation), illustrates how different approaches are helpful for different generations.

- 1950s to 1980s:

  Unchurched ⇨ Present Christ ⇨ Bring into church community ⇨ Join cause

- 1990s to 2000s:

  Unchurched ⇨ Bring into church community ⇨ Present Christ ⇨ Join cause

---

[16] James Emery White, *The Rise of the Nones* (Baker Books, 2014), p. 100.

- Current:

  Unchurched ⇨ Join cause ⇨ Bring into church
  community ⇨ Present Christ

His point being different first points of interest have and do occur as culture changes. My Dutch friend had a cause as her first interest. My validation of her cause within a biblical framework opened up her mind to other aspects of biblical truth.

WORDS, WORKS AND WONDERS

I first became aware of the phrase 'words, works and wonders' through John Wimber. God uses all kinds of ways to reach people and we will be helped in our vision of 'everyone a witness' not by locking everyone into a prescribed system or method, but by seeing the vast and broad range of ways and means God, by His Holy Spirit, draws people to Christ. Our role is to engage with the opportunities God presents us with.

Thomas Brooks observes,

> *"Some are brought to Christ by fire, storms and tempests; others by more easy and gentle gales of the Spirit. The*

Spirit is free in the work of conversion and as the wind, it blows where and how it pleases. Thrice happy are those souls that are brought to Christ, whether it be in a winter's night, or on a summer's day" [17]

WORDS

How then will they call on him in whom they have not believed? And how are they to believe in him of whom they have never heard? And how are they to hear without someone preaching?

ROMANS 10:14 (ESV)

Works and wonders reinforce the authenticity of gospel, but at some point words are required to announce or herald the gospel message. *"Preaching means proclaiming good news. The preacher announces that God's epoch of salvation has arrived. ...Paul is not laying down rigid rules about how people are reached with the gospel of Jesus..."* [18]

---

[17] Charles Haddon Spurgeon, *Smooth Stones Taken From Ancient Brooks* (Banner of Truth, 2011), p. 45.

[18] Michael A. Eaton, *The Branch Exposition of the Bible, Volume 1: A Preacher's Commentary of the New Testament* (Langham Global Library, 2020), p. 492.

I went to church for years feeling a general sense of belief in God but having no clue how to find Him or what a Christian even was. It took the arrival of a new pastor at the church to clearly and simply convey the gospel. Two weeks in and the lights went on and I received Christ. It helps to find a way of speaking about Jesus that feels natural to you.

Again, on a flight, I was in a conversation with the gentleman sitting next to me. As so often happens, the subject of what kind of work we did came up. I said I was a pastor (I think people at least have some understanding of what that means) and he said he was the conductor of a world famous philharmonic orchestra. Alright then.

Noting I was a pastor, he said he was Jewish by background, and then out of the blue he asked me "What do you think it means to be born again?" I have never doubted since then that we can never know what people are processing and what God might be doing in the hidden places of a person's heart. These inner thoughts are often the first stirrings of the Spirit of God in a person.

Without God people rarely give God a thought. If they do, it is soon dismissed and moved on from. We are spiritually dead and incapable of finding God on our own. But the Holy Spirit, unseen by others and maybe even barely recognized by the recipients, begins bringing new birth. Then we can find ourselves, as witnesses, simply aiding what God has already begun. We talk to a person, giving simple opportunities for them to open up further in conversation if they wish. Has anyone asked you a spiritual question recently? Did it surprise you? Maybe God is secretly at work in their heart right now?

I've shared a couple of stories of conversations I've had on aeroplanes but I am quite a shy person and not naturally comfortable at opening up conversations with strangers. I have had to find tools to empower me though still to this day it requires a bit of inner courage to step out.

A BETTER NEW NORMAL

We can always be creative with words. My friend Jimmi Clarke had been through a serious health challenge in his life and wanted to be 'a witness' to the goodness of God in a way that might help others come a step closer to Christ. This is the letter (slightly edited to make sense for a wider audience) he wrote to his street:

Hi, My name's Jim Clarke and I'm a neighbour, I live at number 36 with my wife Emma and our two sons. A couple of years ago I was feeling unwell, so my doctor sent me for some tests. I went thinking I was going to get tablets for a stomach ulcer but I was met by a doctor and three nurses who told me I had cancer. They told me I would need to have chemotherapy and after that they would remove all of my stomach and some of my oesophagus. I was told that life would be very different after surgery and I'd have to get used to a new way of life which they called my 'new normal'.

I was devastated, not only because I'm young, but because I'm a husband and a father to an amazing wife and two amazing kids, who I completely adore. I've been a self-employed musician ever since I was 17. Since then I've toured the world playing bass and I've spent the last 10 years playing for Gloria Gaynor. I didn't know if I'd ever be able to play or tour again. I was gutted as I sat reading through the endless leaflets the nurses gave me. As you can imagine I was super scared about my future, my family and everything that we would have to face.

Amazingly something changed. The worry and fear that seemed so deeply anchored to my soul went away. I was completely filled with peace but not just peace but also hope. Hope for a very uncertain future and more importantly hope for my family. I go to Lowestoft Community Church and have lots of friends who pray and they prayed for me. It was after they prayed that I was completely filled with peace, my fear left me and I was filled with hope. If I did feel scared I'd just text someone from the church and as they prayed the peace and hope would come back. I know this sounds a bit weird and a bit mad but it's true. It's now two years on and I'm completely cancer free!! Whoop! I've been completely discharged. Yep, I lost my stomach and half my oesophagus like the doctor said but my 'new normal' is actually better than the old normal! I've been back working full time for the last 16 months, and last year was financially the best year I'd had in years. I put this down to the prayer I received and also knowing there's a God who could see me, and not just see me but wanted to help me and not punish me. It was this that got me through.

You know if you see a great movie, hear a great band or hear a funny joke, you want to tell someone about it. I've sent this to everyone on our road as I believe if someone does something good for you, you should pay it forward. So I wanted to write to tell you that prayer gave me peace. I just wanted to say if you're going through something difficult, or know someone who is, I'd love to pray for you or them. I'm not a weird religious guy, I'm a bass player who grew up locally. I won't hassle you or knock on your door. But you can knock on my door or send a note through, you can even send a note anonymously if you want. I'm on Facebook too if you want to message me on there. If you feel that this is not for you please feel free to file this letter in the bin.

Many thanks

Jim Clarke

Is there a letter in you, to your street, work colleagues, family or running club? Do you have the words to help you be a witness?

WORKS

Keep your behaviour excellent among the [unsaved] Gentiles [conduct yourself honourably, with graciousness and integrity], so that for whatever reason they may slander you as evildoers, yet by observing your good deeds they may [instead come to] glorify God in the day of visitation [when He looks upon them with mercy].

1 PETER 2:12 (AMP)

We are called to live in such a way that we express and represent God's nature and character. We are "ambassadors", as the Bible puts it. We are those who are sent to represent a higher authority on whose behalf we speak. If we are in a position of work, where we have a PA or front desk representing us or our business, we all would want those our clients and the public first come into contact with to represent us as if we were there ourselves.

For example, the Bible says God is kind. So if we are not kind people then that influences how people view God and the gospel. Kindness is not the end goal, but these qualities authenticate the gospel.

We are not called to change culture, we are called to bring people to the Saviour. As hearts are changed through encounter with God, society naturally feels the benefit.

Great revivals of the past when many came to Christ always brought in their aftermath benefits to the wider society. Being a believer should make you care about social justice and kindness. The more Christian influence within society the better, that society should be run as more righteousness and integrity is exhibited. There should be better work ethics benefiting the economy. The fabric of society, institutions, businesses, the arts all become better for the influence of Christians being involved in them. Large numbers of Christians living a godly lifestyle is simply good news for society.

We cannot right every wrong but each of us is placed within our neighbourhood, church, workplace, circle of friends to express the kindness of God through our 'works'. This is part of 'everyone a witness'.

EMPOWERING THE POOR

So then, as we have opportunity, let us do good to everyone, and especially to those who are of the household of faith.

GALATIANS 6:10 (ESV)

Jesus reminded us we will always have the poor with us and there will never be an end to need. But this verse shows that we each will get opportunities unique to us and our churches to engage with those in various kinds of poverty. Although it is worth noting that we are not to feel the weight of the whole world on our shoulders, we are to be engaged. Consider this testimony from a lady called Nessa.

I had medical help to cope with depression that had set in, but I knew there was still something wrong. In my therapy sessions one of my biggest wishes was to be part of a church, I didn't know why. I wondered what life was about, why it was a constant battle, I couldn't understand what I was fighting for.

Debt problems overtook me, and I (eventually) looked for help. I found Christians Against Poverty (CAP), and two CAP workers from a local church visited me. They prayed with me and I felt something lift immediately. They invited me to come with them to church. I went and instantly when I entered the room, I knew I was in the right place. The feeling of love and acceptance was overwhelming.

I can now live my life the way I want to. God loves me, and I love him. The depression, whilst not gone, is much easier to cope with, and I know why I am alive. Being a Christian has truly saved my life and I'm so thankful for the witness of the CAP workers, who truly helped me find my way to Jesus.

We are to care for both the believer and non-believer. John Calvin wrote:

> *We are not to consider what men merit of themselves but to look upon the image of God in all men, to which we owe all honour and love. However it is among members of the household of faith that this same image is more carefully to be noted (Galatians 6:10) insofar as it has been renewed and restored through the Spirit of Christ. Therefore, whatever man you meet who needs your aid, you have no reason to refuse to help him. … Say that he does not deserve even the least effort for his sake; but the image of God, which recommends him to you, is worthy of giving yourself and all your possessions.*[19]

---

[19] John Calvin, *Institutes of the Christian Religion*, III.7.6. Quoted in a tweet from Timothy Keller, 12.40am, 21 August 2020. www.twitter.com/timkellernyc/status/1296592882187612160

WONDERS

How will we escape if we neglect so great a salvation?
After it was at the first spoken through the Lord, it was
confirmed to us by those who heard, God also testifying
with them, both by signs and wonders and by various
miracles and by gifts of the Holy Spirit according to His
own will.

HEBREWS 2:3-4 (ESV)

For the early part of my Christian life, 'words' were the primary means 'everyone a witness' would have been expressed. 'Works' were a feature of such groups as the Salvation Army. But often in evangelical circles the association of works with the gospel brought fears of the infiltration of a liberal social gospel so working amongst the poor was viewed by many with some caution and seen as the specialty of a few Mother Teresa types. It was only later and gradually that I came to see and experience that 'works' and then 'wonders' also play a crucial part in 'everyone a witness'.

Many of us learnt so much from John Wimber, who I believe was amongst the first to popularise the combination of 'words, works and wonders'. He observed *"Most people respond to acts of mercy and demonstrations of spiritual power"* [20]

Wimber began to show the flow between words and wonders seen in the New Testament. Signs are just that – signs; they point to the truth and authenticity of something. John Wimber helpfully pointed to the teachings of George Eldon Ladd concerning the kingdom:

> *The fact that we are living between the first and the second comings of Christ, what George Ladd calls living between the 'already and the not yet', provides the interpretive key for understanding why the physical healing that Christ secured for us in or through the atonement is not always experienced today.*
>
> *His sovereignty, lordship and kingdom are what bring healing. Our part is to pray, 'Thy Kingdom come' – and to trust him for whatever healing comes from his gracious hand. And if in this age it does not come, then we still*

---

[20] John Wimber with Kevin Springer, *Power Evangelism: Signs and Wonders Today* (Hodder & Stoughton, 1997), p. 73.

have assurance from the atonement that it will come in
the age to come.[21]

Our responsibility now in 'everyone a witness' is to show love, feel compassion and offer to pray with people for healing whenever the opportunity arises. Our part is obedience, God's part is doing the healing. As we step out more and more in this, it is not surprising that we begin to see more people being healed.

One helpful way to get going is to pray in pairs. Jesus sent the disciples out two by two into similar contexts. It can take so much pressure off us personally if we have someone working with us as we pray for people.

If you want your faith built up and encouraged in preparation for stepping out a bit more in praying for people who are unwell, you would do well to watch a number of the extraordinary medically verified healings that take place with regularity at the Newday youth event. Adrian Holloway has

---

[21] John Wimber with Kevin Springer, *Power Healing* (Hodder & Stoughton, 1986, reprinted 2001), p. 169.

repeated the same opportunity for people to encounter God in healing year after year with some remarkable results. [22]

The very worst that can happen if we express things well is that someone feels we cared enough to want to help them. I learnt this once praying for a neighbour. I felt God had given me a prophetic word for her. As I brought the word she started to weep. After I had finished praying I asked, "Did the word make any sense to you?" She replied, "Maybe. I need to think more, but at least I know you care." Her tears were not, on this occasion, due to my remarkable accuracy (though I am still sure it was right) but to the fact I expressed the heart of God for her in caring. It can take quite a bit of courage to first step out in this way. But I encourage you to live intentionally thinking God may begin to bring people along your path during the daily routines of life who He wants you to offer to pray with.

---

[22] Some testimonies of healings at Newday Events are on Adrian's website: www.adrianholloway.com/healing/

5
AN AFRICAN
EQUATOR CROSSING
HELPING PEOPLE CROSS
THE LINE OF FAITH.

My good friend Edward Buria leads a family of churches across various African nations. He is based in Kenya, not far from the equator. I have had the privilege of driving to the equator, getting out of the car and wandering from one hemisphere to the other, telling myself of my new location each time while perplexed locals wonder at this strange 'mzungu' tribal dance. Just as we switch hemispheres when we cross the equator, in this chapter I want to give attention to 'crossing the line' of faith: receiving Christ, and beginning to follow Him.

The New Testament has various expressions for describing the life of someone who has 'crossed the line'; being born again, becoming a Christian, a disciple, a believer, a follower of the Way. Talk to anyone who has received Christ and their account of how it happened will vary. Some can remember a definite moment where everything changed, while for others there was a more gradual growth into awareness that they believe in Christ.

There is no greater merit in a story that says, "I was a rebel and did some terrible things, then God turned my life around," compared to the one that says, "I grew up in a Christian home and can't recall a time when I didn't know Jesus as my Saviour. I grew into a stronger, clearer faith as I grew up." We might even say the less you have to repent of the better!

However it happens, for some it might feel like a small step, yet, as with crossing the equator, so much is different! Winds, tides, seasons and even the constellations of the night sky change. Monumental changes from such a small step.

My friend Edward came to faith in Jesus in January 1975 and that same day he was remarkably healed of a life-threatening heart condition. As a result of what God had done, Edward simply began to start telling his story.

> *I started to witness to people about the miracle I had received and it was evident to the people. We're talking about schools, we're talking about colleges, we're talking about open market places. Just by sharing my testimony I'd see people healed. I'd see the crippled walk, the blind receive their sight, I'd see cancerous wounds being healed, I would see people possessed by evil spirits getting set free just sharing my testimony.*
>
> *This is one of the greatest experiences for me, of the things that God has been able to show me, that has kept me strong in my faith and that has helped me to keep my focus. It tells me even if we pray and we don't see something happening, it doesn't mean that God has lost His power. No! There are thousands of people that came to faith as a result of listening to my testimony!*

This, for Edward, is the evidence of faith – the impact of his testimony about what Jesus has done in his life. And that, in essence, is what this book is all about, encouraging all of us to take regular steps to be a witness to the transforming power of Jesus Christ.

Now, if you're anything like me, you might have become accustomed to receiving such a lukewarm response to your efforts that you'd be surprised if someone said, "Yes, I want to believe in Jesus!"

So what happens then? How can we be sure that those who do want to follow Jesus are genuinely crossing the line from spiritual death in Adam to spiritual life in Christ?

My friend Steve's story is helpful here. Notice what he has done to be ready for the opportunity when it arises.

What I have found helpful over recent years, however, are the "3 Circles" brief presentation of the Bible's Big Story, plus the "15-Second Testimony" which helps me tell my own story within that.

Neither of these have I ever used precisely like the tutorials can tend to teach us, but instead I have been able to use them in an informal manner in conversation whenever openings do arise. In those moments instead I'm storytelling, using the main elements as opposed to reciting scripted lines or giving an overt "teaching moment". This has started to happen increasingly, natural beats in conversation lending themselves far more than I'd realised, and it unlocks conversation far more than I've really experienced before.

One example was when we organised a street WhatsApp group when COVID first hit. Having already been spending years arranging Christmas Drinks and BBQs, with others soon reciprocating, this group was a natural next step. Immediately our neighbours wanted to organise a socially-distanced street party, and we ended up having four of them in 2020. During these, one of our neighbours, who knew we were Christians, told me she was envious of my faith and wanted what we have.

Knowing her well already, I was able to share the Bible's Big Story easily (3 Circles), and then show how my story fitted into that (15-Second Testimony). We had a long conversation on the back of that, which led to a doorstep prayer of commitment to Christ two weeks later and regular Bible study once things began opening up again. She's struggled with many things since then, so it's an up and down walk, but Jesus has certainly started something in her that I have the privilege to walk alongside, and it's been through learning how to tell God's Big Story succinctly, and how my story fits into that, which has enabled this. She isn't the only example, and each time it's been these elements, for me at least, that have helped make the difference.

Let's break down those elements. First, Steve and his family had been intentionally building relationships with his neighbours "for years". Secondly, they took initiative to connect people in challenging situations. Their lives were visible to their neighbours. In that time, Steve took another step and made sure he knew how to tell the gospel and found a couple of tools that worked for him. So when his neighbour's heart was ready, so was Steve!

Everyone who comes to faith in Christ will have a different story of the 'how' the process surrounding it. What each will have in common is a secret work of the Holy Spirit bringing them to birth in Christ; being "born again" as Jesus describes it to an inquiring Nicodemus[23]. There are after all lots of different points and ways you can cross the equator.

THE PLACE OF THIRST

For someone to receive Christ first requires that they are thirsty for spiritual truth. Jesus said in John 3:37, *"If a man is*

---

[23] John 3:7.

84

thirsty let him come to me and drink." If there is no thirst there will be no receiving of Christ because there is no interest.

Jesus, when He sent out the twelve disciples on mission, told them to watch for evidence of thirst. In essence saying "If they receive you and what you have to say, then stay and invest. If they do not then move on to find others who are showing signs of spiritual thirst." The phrase finding "people of peace"[24] is often used today for such scenarios. In other words, finding someone who is open to the messenger and the message. Look for and work with those who are thirsty and open to both you and your message. Bear in mind that someone who presently is not thirsty, might well become thirsty in due course. As we witness to Christ we must observe and work with where each person is at.

In one recent summer, we had a number of tomato plants in the garden and an unusually abundant crop emerging. The ripening process was not uniform, some took much longer than others. We had to wait until they were ripe to pick. We can learn much about complex spiritual matters from

---

[24] Luke 10:6.

observing simple daily life. A similar 'ripening process' is taking place as God works in the hearts of people we seek to witness to. Don't pick fruit that is under-ripe or leave ripe fruit too long. Watch and observe what God is doing. All sorts of providential works of God may be going on in the background that we are totally unaware of. We benefit in our approach to being a witness by trusting that God is working and we play our part as He gives opportunity. He brings us into play at just the right time.

TOWARD BIBLICAL THINKING

In John 3:6-7, Nicodemus presses Jesus about this new birth, looking for greater clarity. Jesus is unequivocal in emphasising that our salvation ultimately comes from and is by the Holy Spirit of God and not from any human activity. *"That which is born of the flesh is flesh, and that which is born of the Spirit is spirit. Do not marvel that I said to you, 'You must be born again.'"*

We have been commissioned to go into all the world and preach the gospel. Paul rightly asks, *"How can they believe unless they hear?"* [25] As we obediently respond to this great commission we look for evidence of thirst, we work with those we see God working upon and as we do this, a supernatural birth, brought about by the sovereign work of the Holy Spirit, occurs. Mysteriously and yet clearly we see the regenerating work of God upon their previously dead spiritual condition and they are brought from death to life. We rejoice that as we have been obedient and done our part, God does what God alone can do – raise the dead to life.

As others have observed, it may take multiple inputs and contacts with Christians before someone comes to Christ. I have not often found myself as the last link and the one who brings the person through to the Lord. I hope that I have more often been one of the links in the process.

One wonderful example of being a link in a chain consider this from my friend Olly Knight, a wedding photographer based in Kent. Olly writes,

> *I received a letter from someone who I'd briefly met at a wedding more than six years previously. I was*

---

[25] Romans 10:14.

photographing at this wedding and in the evening, once the dancing had started, I was having a quick breather outside. There was another person there on their own who was the bride's younger brother. I went up and spoke to him and apparently I chatted to him about God. The wedding took place in a church earlier on that day and I was just asking him about what he thought about God. He was asking me, and I was talking about the love of God and how I love God and have a sense of purpose and all this sort of stuff. The conversation only lasted a few minutes, and I can't even remember the conversation now. But I received this letter where this guy remembered our conversation and it obviously ended up planting a seed in his mind. He thought about it quite a lot and then a few years on, he gives his life to Jesus and decides to send me this letter.

The letter (slightly edited for length and personal details):

Dear Olly,

I am so excited to be able to write you this letter. Yet you undoubtedly have no idea who it is that is writing these words. Allow me to provide an introduction.

Nearly six years ago, you were the photographer at my older sister's wedding: I served as an usher on that day. What you likely do not remember is our brief encounter during the reception once the celebrations and dancing were in full swing. Finding me alone in the grounds of the reception venue, you struck up a conversation in which you made reference to God, your love of Him and a question to me as to my thoughts on belief in God. At the time I was very unreceptive. Oh what foolishness! What ignorance! That I might deny myself the great riches and blessings that God lays before us of a life lived devoted to Him. What stubbornness! What an absolute tragedy and how painful it must have been for you to witness a sinful unbeliever rejecting their living, awesome and powerful everlasting redeemer.

And yet here I am, nearly six years later, writing you this letter. And so, you may be asking why? Well, my dear brother, is it not obvious? I am writing to share with you the greatest news I may ever share with anyone in my life. I have been saved by His amazing grace! I confess with my mouth that Jesus is Lord and believe in my heart that God raised Him from the dead. All glory and honour and praise to Him, our risen Lord!

Now as utterly delightful as it is to share such a magnificent change in my life, that I have truly been re-born in the Holy Spirit, that my past self who was dead to sin is truly dead, what I wish to do now is this: offer my heartfelt thanks to you.

You see, whilst our conversation may have seemed brief and altogether one devoid of preaching the good news to someone ready to receive it, it stuck with me over the years. Through my own personal struggles and of the true depths of despair, your little conversation, along with the little conversations of many other Christian brothers and sisters, sowed a seed of peace in my heart. And now you are reaping a harvest of righteousness for the glory of God's kingdom. So, I say again: Thank you! Might this short letter be a reminder to you to always be full of joy in the Lord. I say it again – rejoice! Let everyone see that you are considerate in all you do. For you do not know how many further seeds of peace you might still sow throughout your life, through the simplest, most insignificant of interaction. Those seeds, however small, may fall on fertile soil. And if they do, how very significant are those interactions to the person who might be saved through them. May you and your family remain blessed, safe and wrapped in the warmth of God's love, forever and always. And may the grace of the Lord Jesus Christ be with your spirit.

Did you notice how he described the links in the chain? *"Your little conversation, along with the little conversations of many other Christians brothers and sisters, sowed a seed of peace in my heart."*

We do not have to get someone 'over the line' – crossing the equator of conversion – each time we witness for Christ. We make our contribution, obediently taking the opportunities available to us. It is 'everyone a witness' that enables many people to come to Christ. We are called to be fruitful, not productive. Productivity-thinking focuses on, "How many have I got over the line?" Fruitfulness-thinking is, "Have I been an obedient witness and a good ambassador of Christ?"

John Newton sums it up well: *"He found us when we sought him not. Then we began to seek him, and he was pleased to be found by us."* [26]

---

[26] From John Newton's letters via a tweet from @john__newton, 1.10pm, 31 October 2019.
www.twitter.com/john__newton/status/1189892494122737665

6

A SCHOOL IN NORWICH

THE GOAL IS TO BE MATURE IN CHRIST

*As I remember, we went down the aisle, up by the organ
and up a staircase into the schoolroom, which was packed
with inquirers; they were not all young people but older
as well. That was the night when I first knew what it was
to have faith in Christ. I knew very little, just as every
new convert knows very little, but I knew sufficient of the
facts and I had trusted Christ as my Saviour.[27]*

So spoke a young convert from my hometown during the
1921 Lowestoft revival. Many years later, when I came to
Christ, also in the same town, my reflection was I also knew
very little but that I had received Christ and given my life to
Him.

Terry Virgo was conducting a national tour, affectionately
known as the 'EGG' tour (Enjoying God's Grace). The East

---

[27] Stanley Griffin, *A Forgotten Revival* (Day One, 2001), p. 23.

Anglian leg saw many gather in a school in Norwich. I cannot recall ever hearing more liberating preaching. I had grown up around quite a legalistic version of church life: "Don't play football on a Sunday", "Don't talk in church", "Always confess sin first so God is then ready to hear you". This Christianity is summed up as, "You are basically disappointing to God but His love has just about saved you. But don't ever get too over-confident about that as you are only one day away from sinning again and going all the way back down the ladder and having to climb your way back up to earn something like an acceptable amount of approval in your standing with God."

Terry proceeded to 'blast' lots of legalistic nonsense out of the water through careful, detailed exposition especially of key passages and principles in Romans with then hugely liberating application to the Christian life.[28]

---

[28] Terry Virgo, 'Grace, Parts 1-3', 2nd-4th October 2011, www.terryvirgo.org

GREATER ILLUMINATION HELPS US WITNESS

In the last chapter, I talked about crossing the line of faith and sometimes Christians have put all their focus and energies on that moment and then done very little. I would suggest the Bible does not think in that way. We are looking to make disciples. People who follow Christ, learn from Christ and serve Christ.

I can honestly say Terry's teaching changed my life as a believer. I now had a grasp of how good the good news was. No longer was I motivated in my Christian life out of a mix of duty and joy.

I previously had a simple awareness that the gospel was true and people needed saving. But I realised now just how much the gospel was 'good news' not just to get us to heaven but to live life in a totally liberated way through what Christ had achieved here and now. God does not want saved-but-totally-condemned witnesses running around. He wants us to know more of what this salvation means, which cannot help but motivate us to speak more of it.

This is not a one-off thing; we constantly need our own hearts refocused on amazing truths that liberate us. Like putting the windscreen wipers on and realising just how restricted the view was. When did you last switch the wipers on and see afresh the truths of God's wonderful grace for yourself?

GREATER MOTIVATION HELPS US WITNESS

When we go to a good football game, hear a great piece of music or enjoy an evening at a wonderful restaurant, we naturally want to tell people about it. Experiencing the reality of something motivates the telling of it more than simply reading it from a book or hearing accounts of it from someone else.

If we want the vision of 'everyone a witness' to become a reality we need to grasp more and more the greatness of our salvation. In other words we have to truly grasp how good the good news is. We will then, I hope, be more excited to tell others of what has touched us with such great power.

We are not selling vacuum cleaners, we are 'witnesses' to something that has changed our lives. *"Jesus said to those Jews who had believed him, 'If you continue in my word, then you are truly disciples of mine; and you will know the truth, and the truth will make you free.'"* [29]

The truth does set us free, but not just truth; truth applied. We must "continue" as the verses say. We do not need fundamentally new techniques of witness. We may well need greater illumination in our hearts of the salvation we have been given.

> *For out of the overflow of the heart the mouth speaks.*
>
> LUKE 6:45 (ESV)

> *Therefore I tell you, her sins, which are many, are forgiven—for she loved much. But he who is forgiven little, loves little.*
>
> LUKE 7:47 (ESV)

To be forgiven much does not always mean having a greater volume of wrongdoing but simply a deep awareness of the

---

[29] John 8:31-32 (ESV).

effect of even one sin and the remedy required to bring about forgiveness. After all, it only took one sin for Adam to afflict death and sin upon humanity.

I want to be for things not against them. I want new believers to learn that there are secondary issues that Christians have different opinions about but that we love, respect and learn from the grace of God on others. I want new believers to learn that there is mystery at times concerning the Christian life, that dogma is not always appropriate in matters of biblical interpretation.

However, I also want them to know that there are foundational truths which, when embraced, will give such strength to the new believer seeking to grow in Christ. This list is not exhaustive but I would say over the years these issues tend to come up again and again, as things key to helping those coming to Christ come also to maturity in their faith.

GRACE AND IDENTITY ISSUES

"Who am I" and "Where do I fit" are huge questions, especially in the individualistic West. More collectivist cultures find the answer to those questions more easily in group identity. When they come to Christ they readily see themselves as finding a place in another 'family', God's new 'people' or 'tribe' on the Earth. They quickly grasp the truth of one new humanity 'in Christ'.

> *And the free gift is not like the result of that one man's sin. For the judgement following one trespass brought condemnation, but the free gift following many trespasses brought justification. For if, because of one man's trespass, death reigned through that one man, much more will those who receive the abundance of grace and the free gift of righteousness reign in life through the one man Jesus Christ. Therefore, as one trespass led to condemnation for all men, so one act of righteousness leads to justification and life for all men. For as by the one man's disobedience the many were made sinners, so by the one man's obedience the many will be made righteous.*

> ROMANS 5:16-19 (ESV)

Anyone who has felt the effects of a detention of the whole class at school because of the actions of one person can glimpse something of our condition before coming to know Christ. As Dr Martyn Lloyd-Jones writes, *"By one man's disobedience we were put into the category of sinners, we were constituted sinners."*[30]

It is important to know that before Christ our identity was "in Adam". That single piece of knowledge helps us grasp that we have had a change of identity now that we are "in Christ".

> *As Adam's one act of disobedience has constituted us all sinners, so the obedience of the Lord Jesus Christ constitutes all who believe in him as righteous, and justifies them by faith…. On the one hand Adam's sin is imputed to us; on the other, Christ's righteousness is imputed to us.*[31]

Words such as "justified" and "imputed" and the meaning they carry matter hugely. It is important to grasp that God has removed our guilt and sin and gifts us now with the gift of Christ's righteousness. He removed our sinfulness and guilt because He took them upon Himself on the cross and in doing so declared us to be righteous. As Martin Luther put it,

---

[30] Martyn Lloyd-Jones, *Assurance: Romans 5* (Banner of Truth Trust, 1971), p. 209.

[31] Ibid, pp. 209-210.

This is that mystery which is rich in divine grace to sinners: wherein by a wonderful exchange our sins are no longer ours but Christ's, and the righteousness of Christ not Christ's but ours. He has emptied himself of his righteousness that he might clothe us with it and fill us with it; and he has taken our evils upon himself that he might deliver us from them.[32]

If that were not enough. God shows us that justification was the means to His greater intended goal, which is adoption. God could have saved us, forgiven us and kept us at a lower level of relationship. It is not essential for the legal system for a judge acquitting the accused to then adopt them into their family. Thus God could have forgiven us but remained distant and detached from us. However, adoption was always His goal. Justification was the means essential to secure it.

Ephesians 1:5 says, *"he predestined us for adoption to himself as sons through Jesus Christ, according to the purpose of his will..."*

To quote J.I.Packer on this theme, he asks:

---

[32] Martin Luther, *Werke* (Weimar, 1883), Vol. 5, p. 608, via www.tollelege.net/2009/11/19/a-wonderful-exchange-by-martin-luther/

What is the highest privilege of the gospel? What is a Christian? The question can be answered in many ways, but the richest answer I know is that a Christian is one who has God as Father.

If you want to judge how well a person understands Christianity, find out how much they make of the thought of being God's child, and having God as their Father. If this is not the thought that prompts and controls their worship and prayers and whole outlook on life, it means that they do not understand Christianity very well at all.

Adoption… is the highest privilege that the gospel offers: higher even than justification… To be right with God the Judge is a great thing, but to be loved and cared for by God the Father is a greater.[33]

EMPOWERMENT ISSUES

These truths on identity help a new believer grasp that they are now dead to sin – it does not reign over them any longer. They have a new identity, they can say "no" to sin and "yes" to righteousness. Not only do we have a new identity but we

---

[33] J.I. Packer, *Knowing God* (Hodder & Stoughton, 1976), pp. 200-201, 206.

have a renewed nature. We are "new creations". How does this happen? Well, because just as the Father sent His Son, so His Son sends the Spirit to dwell with us. God Himself now lives in us, by His Spirit, empowering us to live the Christian life. We do not need to struggle with constant sin or failure in thought, word or deed any longer. We can become all God intends us to be. The Holy Spirit works in us to help us become who we actually are. Just as our old way of life matched our old identity so our new way of life should match our new identity.

Sanctification is the word that theologians use to describe this process of being changed more and more into the likeness of Christ. This is our true identity "in Christ". To bear the family likeness, to resemble Christ who was the image of the invisible God.

Now we all still live with an as-yet unredeemed body with all its appetites, pulls and dysfunctions. Our nature is now fundamentally new. It is alive to God and dead to sin. We are not merely reformed creations but new ones. Jesus does not just merely improve us and then help us self-improve some more. We are spiritually alive when before we were spiritually dead. We were incapable of pleasing God or saving ourselves by any merit of work of our own. Now we naturally want to please God. A resurrection miracle has taken place. We need not have to sin any longer, it does not have dominion over us through identity.

If God can raise a dead man to life He can raise our dead natures to life through the same Spirit dwelling in us. We are not defeated, trying to limp along, we are 'reigning in life' through Christ; this is a position and condition not an aspiration longed for.

SECURITY OF SALVATION ISSUES

I have two books on my shelves, one called *Once Saved, Always Saved* by RT Kendall, the other *Once Saved, Always Saved?* by David Pawson. The question mark at the end of the second title reveals that although both books address the same theme, both come to different conclusions.

To nail my colours to the mast on this matter (though I would encourage you to read both books and think for yourself) I am biblically persuaded no question mark is necessary.

To quote RT Kendall summarising this doctrine,

> *Whoever once truly believes that Jesus was raised from the dead, and confesses that Jesus is Lord, will go to heaven when he dies.... Such a person will go to heaven when he dies no matter what work (or lack of work) may accompany such faith.*[34]

A genuine conversion is evidenced by fruit in keeping with the new birth. There are things that are evidence of the new nature at work in us. As James says, *"faith without works is dead"* [35]. Pears naturally grow on a pear tree.

However, the honest truth is that we can fluctuate in our spiritual life; not every day is better than the one that went before it. Yet in the life of someone born again of the Spirit of God even when various spiritual ups and downs happen, even backsliding, it might be almost impossible to see evidence of spiritual life whilst a wilderness time ensues. Jesus tells the famous story of the prodigal son and while he wasn't always a

---

[34] RT Kendall, *Once Saved, Always Saved* (Hodder & Stoughton, 1984), p. 16.
[35] James 2:17.

prodigal he was always a son, even if he didn't look or behave like one.

But in the end the new nature – the life of God, the indwelling of the Holy Spirit – cannot help but show itself.

Taking a position on whether someone is 'saved' or not based purely on their present lifestyle can simply degenerate into another way of assessing salvation on the basis of works observed here and now.

People can, of course, learn behaviours in church and through being around Christians. They can learn how to look and sound like the genuine thing but have had no real saving encounter with Christ in their hearts. Likewise the genuinely saved can, in bad seasons, outwardly present an appearance far from what we might assume to be from a believer. Appearances both ways can be misleading.

DECEPTION ISSUES

New believers attract enemy attention. If the enemy cannot prevent their salvation, then he will seek to distort or warp it into something less than correct. We simply cannot leave new Christians without discipleship. We cannot leave people to find their own way, hoping all will be well. That would be like leaving a young child who cannot read and has no money outside a supermarket with a shopping list saying "go, feed yourself".

Young believers are often like sponges; they will listen to and watch anything as they are hungry to learn and grow. I have often made it my business to watch which friendships new believers form. *"Bad company corrupts good character"* says 1 Corinthians 15:33 and I want to do my best to give special attention to young believers.

The world is full of false teachings, lies and half-truths and sadly all too often so is the church, so we need to be on our guard. We need to remember that if the church does not disciple those who come to Christ then someone else, with teachings you don't believe to be biblical, will.

7
A HIGH STREET
RECORD SHOP
COST, CLARITY AND CHANGE

The day finally came, it had been much anticipated and much talked about. It was the day of the latest album release of our hero. My friends met outside the "Record buy and exchange" shop arriving just before opening time, hoping they would not sell out before it was our turn. The questions buzzed around, "What would the new incarnation be?" Would I feel once again that I had found someone, something to identify with, someone who expressed the emotions I felt or was happy to embrace as my own? Life as an ardent David Bowie fan was always about way more than the music. It was an alternative reality to join in with, a world view to embrace. Shaping, calming, affirming, defining and legitimising inner conflicts and questions that simply could not be talked about to anyone, except maybe to other fans – it was always intensely personal.

When I heard the gospel and received Christ I'm not sure I fully realised just what the cost also involved was. As I began to read the Bible and ponder what I was reading, I became thirsty for more. I wanted to please God, to really be the 'real deal', to convict me and agitate my conscience.

BOWIE OR JESUS?

Over time the Holy Spirit began to increasingly work in my life. And all along the way, I felt Him pointing out to me areas of life – thoughts, behaviour patterns, activities, perspectives, possessions and priorities – that were not in keeping with or helping me grow into who I now was. I was in Christ now. A residence of His Spirit. I was a new creation, actually spiritually dead to my old identity and alive in Christ.

So the day came when I drove to the local rubbish depot, got out of my car, and walked towards the skip with all my carefully packaged albums in hand. But I could not throw them in, that felt, well, wrong – vicious somehow. So I gently let them slide down into the recesses of the skip next to the broken furniture and twisted metal. A silent moment fell as I stared at what I had just done. All the Bowie albums, gone. That was a costly decision.

Now you may ask, if there is anything inherently wrong with owning David Bowie LP's? And the answer is "Nothing inherently". But for me these represented a competing God – David Bowie was, quite literally, an idol to me. And he had a way of life that was not the way of Christ. So, for me, it had to be Bowie or Jesus, there was no room for both.

Years later I can listen to Bowie music and it no longer challenges my conscience. It does not represent for me now what it did then. I have outgrown its lure and appeal. I still enjoy the music and I'd probably still be a great asset on a quiz team on his life and work.

What's the point? When we think of ourselves as a witness, it means being a witness to the fact that Jesus is not an accessory to life. We are not inviting people to add Jesus on and try it out to see if He helps. Rather we are inviting people to surrender everything they are and have to His complete

Lordship. We entrust everything to Him and relinquish the right to be in control any longer of anything. That costs us!

TWO TRUTHS

The New Testament, to simplify massively, has two kinds of truths. There are indicatives, these are statements of the things that God has done for us. Like this one:

> *Even when we were dead in our trespasses, made us alive together with Christ – by grace you have been saved.*
>
> EPHESIANS 2:5 (ESV)

Then there are the imperatives, these are things that, if we accept the truths of the indicatives, we embrace as actions. Like this:

> *Put off your old self, which belongs to your former manner of life and is corrupt through deceitful desires, and to be renewed in the spirit of your minds, and to put on the new self, created after the likeness of God in true righteousness and holiness.*
>
> EPHESIANS 4:22-24 (ESV)

110

Now, not all the change that is needed happens at once but still we can pray this old Puritan prayer, *"While Jesus is representing me in Heaven, may I reflect him on earth..."*[36]

If nothing changes in our lives as a result of what we believe then it's not unreasonable to ask ourselves some tough questions. Receiving Christ should bring about change. There are *"things that accompany salvation".*[37]

Having introduced you to indicatives and imperatives I want to introduce another pair of important words: Lord and Saviour. This is how all Christians describe Jesus. He is our Saviour and He is our Lord. That means it is Jesus who is in charge now and not me and not you. When it comes to how we live our lives there is someone else calling the shots now.

Which leads me to my final pair of words that are important: converts and disciples. The one leads to the other. We convert from believing one thing to believing a new thing. We make a shift. And the Bible describes these shifts in powerful ways:

---

[36] Arthur Bennett, The Valley of Vision (Banner of Truth, 1975, reprinted 2019), p. 11.

[37] Hebrews 6:9 (NASB).

darkness to light, death to life, old to new and so on. But not everyone seems to make that shift. Some people accept the indicatives and along the way forget the imperatives.

If 'everyone a witness' is to be anything more than a passing fad this means pointing out to people the following: if you believe the indicatives about Jesus as Saviour and convert that means becoming his disciple. And that means accepting Him as Lord and working out the imperatives in your life. He is not an accessory or an emergency resource. We risk churches full of nominal Christian commitment, if we aim for anything less than this.

As Charles Swindoll brilliantly portrays in his *Pearl of Great Price*:

> *"I want this pearl. How much is it?"*
> *"Well," the seller says, "it's very expensive"*
> *"But, how much?" we ask.*
> *"Well, a very large amount."*
> *"Do you think I could buy it?"*
> *"Oh, of course, everyone can buy it."*
> *"But, didn't you say it was very expensive?"*
> *"Yes."*
> *"Well, how much is it?"*

"Everything you have," says the seller.

We make up our minds, "All right, I'll buy it," we say.

"Well, what do you have?" he wants to know. "Let's write it down."

"Well, I have ten thousand dollars in the bank."

"Good, ten thousand dollars. What else?"

"That's all. That's all I have....well, I have a few dollars here in my pocket."

"How much?"

We start digging. "Well, let's see... thirty, forty, sixty, eighty, a hundred, a hundred twenty dollars."

"That's fine. What else do you have?"

"Well, nothing. That's all."

"Where do you live?" He's still probing.

"In my house. Yes, I have a house."

"The house, too, then." He wrote that down.

"You mean I have to live in my camper?"

"You have a camper? That, too. What else?"

"I'll have to sleep in my car!"

"You have a car?"

"Two of them."

"Both become mine, both cars. What else?"

"Well, you already have my money, my house, my camper, my cars. What more do you want?"

"Are you alone in this world?"

"No, I have a wife and two children....."
"Oh, yes, your wife and children, too. What else?"
"I have nothing left! I am left alone now."
Suddenly the seller exclaims
"Oh, I almost forgot! You, yourself, too! Everything becomes mine, wife, children, house, money, cars, and you too."

Then he goes on. *"Now listen, I will allow you to use all these things for the time being. But don't forget that they are mine, just as you are. And whenever I need any of them you must give them up, because now I am the owner."* [38]

THE CHRISTIAN BIRTH

In the early 1980s, when I was fairly recently converted and having had encounters with the Holy Spirit, myself and a number of friends under the leadership of Ian Savory founded Waveney Youth for Christ. We learnt much about evangelism and over a number of years saw quite an effective program of

---

[38] Juan Carlos Ortiz, *Disciple* (Wheaton, IL: Creation House, 1975), pp. 34-35 as quoted in Charles R Swindoll, *Improving Your Serve* (W Publishing Group, 1981), pp. 35-36.

outreach emerge. We organised everything from Christian rock bands to schools' work to an escapologist. They were heady days wanting to see younger people in our area reached with the gospel and seeing the impact.

However, one event stands out for me that was for the churches in the town. David Pawson, the renowned Bible teacher, was doing a tour called "Let God speak" so we filled a local theatre called "The Sparrows Nest" with around 800 people. As a comedian quipped later, "must have been a very big Sparrow!" That evening was, as my wife describes it, "a gear change for us".

David spoke of the "Normal Christian Birth".[39] His main point was that the New Testament shows four ingredients in the lives of new believers.

- Repentance – turning from sin to Christ and living a new life under His Lordship
- Faith – trusting Christ alone for Salvation as a gift of grace received through faith

---

[39] See: David Pawson, *The Normal Christian Birth* (Hodder & Stoughton, 1991).

- Baptism in water – the first act of obedience taken by a new believer in Christ was to be immersed in water symbolising death to their old life and rising in the new life that is there is now in Christ

- Baptism in the Holy Spirit – whilst we are born again and indwelt by the Holy Spirit in conversion there is a separate or attendant infilling of the Holy Spirit promised to us that should be received when we come to Christ for the empowerment of believers in serving and growing in grace and knowledge of God.

What was so crucial for those of us hearing this teaching was the realisation that though we often saw many people fill in cards, put up hands or come to the front of meetings, it was by no means the case that they all began or grew from that moment. As a result of this and also the woefully inadequate state of the receiving churches many drifted away never to be seen again. We learned that discipleship and good foundations are necessary for future health and a culture of 'everyone a witness'.

THE PERSONAL WORK OF THE HOLY SPIRIT

The great agent of change in our lives is God the Holy Spirit.

> *And I am sure of this, that he who began a good work in you will bring it to completion at the day of Jesus Christ.*
>
> PHILIPPIANS 1:6 (ESV)

This great truth should give us great security and stir up in us a desire to follow the Lord all the more rather than a passivity of "Well if He is going to do it I don't need to bother". The Holy Spirit is at work in all who He brings to new life in Christ. As such, whilst having good foundations and being in a good local church really do aid and nurture our life as believers, at heart the life of God is within us. The Holy Spirit can, does and always will bring about change in us so we become more Christ-like. People, once saved, can change and this change is wrought through and by the Holy Spirit.

We don't want dependency on human beings first but instead a reliance, surrender and dependency on the Holy Spirit for all progress in the life of a believer.

117

SCRIPTURE

> *Think over what I say, for the Lord will give you understanding in everything.*

2 TIMOTHY 2:7 (ESV)

The place for meditating on Scripture or, as Luther put it, *"allowing my thoughts to go for a walk with the Holy Spirit"*[40] is the privilege of sons and daughters of our Father in heaven. To walk with God, our Father, asking Him, listening to Him and learning from Him is part of bringing people to Christ. 'Everyone a witness' is not about introducing people to a set of beliefs but an invitation to embrace a relationship.

> *But the anointing that you received from him abides in you, and you have no need that anyone should teach you.*

1 JOHN 2:27 (ESV)

This is not saying we should not be teachable. The context of the verse is to believers who are being taught that they need a 'special revelation' from teachers who have a hidden

---

[40] Martin Luther, *A Simple Way to Pray*, as quoted in Timothy Keller, *Prayer* (Hodder & Stoughton, 2014), p. 251.

knowledge that they can only access from them. We can each hear God for ourselves; we do not need to go through another human being to access God or hear from God.

THE LOCAL CHURCH

> *And the Lord added to their number day by day those who were being saved.*
>
> ACTS 2:47 (ESV)

'Everyone a witness' means that those coming to Christ are 'saved and added' to the local church where they live. This was how it was in the early church and how it should be today. When Jesus gave the great commission this was, if you like, the first round of 'everyone a witness'.

> *Jesus came and said to them, "All authority in heaven and on earth has been given to me. Go therefore and make disciples of all nations, baptising them in the name of the Father and of the Son and of the Holy Spirit, teaching them to observe all that I have commanded you. And behold, I am with you always, to the end of the age.*
>
> MATTHEW 28:18-20 (ESV)

What is of note here is that the disciples, in their outworking of Jesus' commission, preached the gospel through words, works and wonders. They also planted locally-led churches. They did not stop at leading people to Christ, but built them into communities of faith with God-appointed leadership. It seemed instinctive to them; a natural outworking of the great commission given to reach people with the gospel.

Communities of discipleship and teaching, prayer, fellowship, care for the poor, celebration of the sacraments as part of corporate worship are engine rooms of further witness into the local vicinity. And from there it spreads to the ends of the Earth with a glorious vision for all nations to be reached for Christ. This captured the heart of the early church and it should capture ours today.

Whether we're talking about smaller communities dispersed through persecution or of great gatherings that catch the attention of whole cities and regions, the wineskin of the local church is a vital place to be for the development and maturing of the new wine of people who come to Christ.

The Church is a noun not a verb. It is a local physical and visible thing. We don't 'do' church, we *are* church. We cannot separate evangelism from building the local church without doing damage to the progress of both as well as to the spiritual wellbeing of individual believers. Not only will we not grow well without others, we can also become spiritually unwell.

SERVING MAKES US GROW

We make a mistake if we bring people to Christ only to feel satisfied having them sit week by week listening to perhaps-great Bible teaching but do not train, equip and create structures for releasing them to be a witness for Christ throughout their life. People do not have to be 'ready' to share the gospel. If Christ has done something genuine in their lives, we simply must encourage them to tell others and to show others by how they now serve Christ with their gifts and live their daily lives.

Character and maturity comes in the Christian life as people begin to serve. Employing our gifts and living for Christ draws us into reliance on Him, it creates a hunger for His purpose and stirs motivation to see vision achieved. Personally I am convinced that people who come to Christ need to start serving straight away.

I would observe that a trend not to be discounted in recent years has been termed 'belonging before believing'. People have noted that as people explore the gospel through connection to the church and interaction with the life of God through His people they begin to help out in simple ways. As that happens they begin to find more and more that their hearts are open to the people and to the message. In western cultures, especially where cynicism and scepticism about the church has become more prevalent often through moral or leadership failings, it is not unreasonable for the need for trust to be re-established.

For new believers to be in an environment of fellowship helps their spiritual growth as a disciple. Through watching and learning from others, as well as from good Bible exposition, people broaden their own perspectives on faith and Christian living. It helps us learn vital skills in doing life with others, handling conflicts, clashes and misunderstandings; we learn to think of others and not just ourselves. We start living for the greater good of the whole, not just what is in it for me. We gain from the encouragement or challenges we receive from others as we live together in God's family.

8
A TALE OF TWO AUDITORIUMS

THE GLOBAL PURPOSES OF CHRIST

In 1983, the group of us that comprised the WYFC (Waveney Youth for Christ) committee took what seems in retrospect a huge step of faith. We were mostly in our late teens or early twenties, with more vision than experience. We had a passion to reach our town and surrounding area with the gospel. The vision was to mobilise local churches to engage in 'everyone a witness' by inviting friends, family and colleagues to this mission event.

We rented the local 750 seat Marina theatre for three weeks aiming to host a "Down to Earth" mission with the evangelist Eric Delve. The theatre had seen better days and was only being used as a cinema at the time. Apparently no one had trod the boards of the stage since Vera Lynn in World War Two. We set to work renovating, decorating, cleaning and making good this wonderful jewel of a building. Whilst we did not fill the building completely every night, we did on a number of nights during the three weeks. Certainly, every evening several hundreds of people came and heard the gospel, and many responded to the gospel over the three weeks. Some conversions were quite dramatic.

35 years later I found myself in another nearly full auditorium, again with around 750 seats. Friends House in Euston, London was the scene for our *Relational Mission* family of churches' Leadership & 20s' conference. This time leaders and those in their 20s hungry to serve God descended upon the capital of the UK for the best part of a week. During the week, in the midst of Bible teaching, seminars, worship gatherings and casting vision for our collective apostolic advance, teams went out in pairs in the surrounding streets seeking to share the gospel with words, works and wonders with people God led them to.

'Everyone a witness' will grow from a small start.

35 years lay between these two events from 1983-2018. Much had developed in between, what a journey! God always seems to like starting small. From one person, a few people, one church, one town to multiple towns and locations, many people, many churches, multiplied mission into multiple nations. There is a mustard seed principle built into how God works in and through us. Never be discouraged with small starts or what seems like slow progress at times. There is a relentless advance and fruitfulness built into the way God's kingdom grows. We can learn much from the rhythm of the seasons and God's creation around us. There is, as Ecclesiastes chapter 3 says, *'a time for every purpose under heaven'*.

Do you feel a longing to see much fruit for God in and through your life? Trust God to work out your obedient posture through the principle of the mustard seed.

We can wonder "What does my contribution to witness make? There are so many people to reach, disciples to train. I often don't take the opportunities, I often don't feel I do it well, I don't always know what happens after I have witnessed, I don't see the results and I can't follow everyone up as well as

I want. Can my seemingly small attempts really make any difference?"

Trust God and just take the next step. Obedience is our responsibility, fruitfulness comes from the Lord. I have had more occasions where my attempts to witness and disciple have fallen short of my intended standard than not. I will determine to trust God with my simple attempts at obedience, whilst adopting a humble learning posture all the time learning how to be more effective.

God will bless our earnest, wholehearted efforts of obedience to His calling. We do not aim at productivity, rather we aim at fruitfulness. The first orientates itself by numbers, the second by obedience to God. The first feels time pressure, the second knows God has times, seasons and rhythms which He desires us to watch for and cooperate with.

'EVERYONE A WITNESS' IS CORE BUSINESS

We must never make evangelism a separate department but place it right at the heart of all vision for the local church. In London we put witness right at the heart of what could have been an insular leadership conference. It was a statement about our DNA. Two gatherings (one in Lowestoft and one in London), two different vehicles, one desire for 'everyone a witness'. We must not lose that and in fact we must press into it more.

If there is one thing that comes from this book may it be a resolve not to extract or compartmentalise evangelism, mission and witness as separate from church life or church planting as a kind of department. The same is true for corporate prayer.[41]

Back in the 80s we started to see fresh life brought into the churches as a result of mission. But most churches were far from ready to embrace and disciple new believers. So many New Testament values had been lost and as a result many who had come to Christ could not cope with church and it felt irrelevant to them and their needs. My eyes were opened after reading Terry Virgo's book *Restoration in the Church*. I caught a glimpse of the fact that the Church was supposed to be a

---

[41] See www.prayersofmany.org for more details on corporate prayer.

glorious visible demonstration of God dwelling with His people. So much work needed to be done. I have given much of the past 35 years to a diligent attempt at seeking to restore New Testament values, teaching and doctrine to the local churches I have had the joy of working with.

The impact of that, being perfectly honest, was that so much of my effort went on trying to re-lay foundations of New Testament church life that 'everyone a witness' at times was relegated to "we must get round to that" one day. My creative and strategic eye has at times been taken off mission and requires a firm swing back to mission without losing the ground we have gained in local church renewal and restoration. What I note from the apostle Paul is that he seemed to have walked with a dual focus on both his mission to bring people to Christ and his calling to plant and strengthen local churches. Surely this must also be our dual focus?

EVERYONE A WITNESS AS A FOUNDATION IN THE LOCAL CHURCH

When our local church planted into Great Yarmouth, a town some 10 miles north, one of our elders went to head up the work and he made a wise strategic move. Around 30 or so people went with him to plant the church and he decided that rather than disperse their energies on many projects and activities they would focus on just one: the Alpha Course.[42] Everyone got involved, whether cooking, table hosting, welcoming, inviting or clearing up afterwards. In this way an evangelistic foundation was put in early into this local church plant that was not lost as the church grew. Everyone had got the message that we are here for the mission. Whilst I do not know exact numbers, I believe I am right in saying through this strategy, in the first 18 months of that young church plant, around 70 people came to Christ through the Alpha Course.

---

[42] www.alpha.org

'EVERYONE A WITNESS' NEEDS THE GIFT OF THE EVANGELIST

For many years the church has been happy to use words like pastor and teacher. However the gifts listed in Ephesians 4 are broader than this. Apostle, prophet and evangelist are also gifts of the ascended Christ for the equipping and maturing of the church. Thankfully, through careful exegesis and well thought-through application we are seeing a restoration of these gifts globally across the church. The church will never become all she is intended to be without receiving these gifts; their stated function assigned by the Lord Himself is to equip the saints for service.

An evangelist will have a reaping aspect to their gift; by that I mean that the gift of an evangelist will be seen by people regularly coming to Christ. They will also have a grace on them to make everyone else in the church feel empowered, encouraged and enabled to also lead people to Christ. I recall a Sunday when Adrian Holloway, himself a significant reaping evangelist, came to our local church to share on being an effective witness. I left church having never felt so empowered to witness. Most people, I think, came away thinking "I can actually do this, and I am keen to have a go."

Being hit over the head by "ought to" does nothing to equip. We need more evangelists like Adrian, who reap but also encourage and equip the church. Identifying and releasing these grace gifts amongst the church is a huge part of creating the culture of 'everyone a witness'. If you get too close to an evangelist, their anointing will rub off on you and the water level of your desire to witness will rise. If you are in leadership in a local church, make strategic plans to have an evangelist come to your church to help not only demonstrate reaping but to equip and encourage the whole church to be witnesses for Christ.

There is something about the atmosphere and the momentum created by an Ephesians 4 gift serving into a local church or family of churches. An evangelist, without exception, somehow over time and in the right context, produces a culture change and fruitfulness in collective witness.

'EVERYONE A WITNESS' MEANS LEARNING AS WE GO

> *To those outside the law I became as one outside the law (not being outside the law of God but under the law of Christ) that I might win those outside the law. To the weak I became weak, that I might win the weak. I have become all things to all people, that by all means I might save some.*

1 CORINTHIANS 9:21-22 (ESV)

There is no 'best' method of sharing the gospel. The vehicle of delivery can and should vary according to the context and culture being reached. Over the years effective methods have arisen to suit various times and settings.

I have seen effectiveness from open-air preaching, street witness, gospel preaching, music and the arts, unusual testimonies of people who have found Christ, converted buses traveling town to town, phone-in 'helplines', addiction rehab ministry programs, people remarkably gifted at communicating the gospel to children, beach missions, kids clubs, Sunday schools, discussion style courses such as Alpha or Christianity Explored, door-to-door visitation and leafleting, online services, tent and stadium crusades, one-to-one witness to strangers, neighbours, friends or colleagues, Bible story telling in oral cultures, discovery Bible studies in reaching people from a Muslim background. Plus many more besides.

Paul expresses a desire to be creative, attentive, experimental and relevant to whatever audience he finds a door of opportunity in. We can learn from so many and use the vehicles developed. My hope is that maybe people reading this may as yet create new vehicles to reach new contexts helping see 'everyone a witness'.

Our chief calling is to be custodians of the gospel in our generation so that the generations to come have the gospel passed to them with integrity preserved. Ensuring the inheritance of the church is not lost to a coming generation. We must take this charge most seriously. We find a sobering observation of a next generation in Judges 2:10 (ESV):

> *And all that generation also were gathered to their fathers. And there arose another generation after them who did not know the LORD or the work that he had done for Israel.*

133

'EVERYONE A WITNESS' AND GOD'S GLOBAL PURPOSES

God has made promises concerning His global purposes and these dictate what we can expect and what will happen.

Expect too much and it can stimulate disappointment, disillusionment and cynicism. Expect too little and it might cause us to become apathetic to sharing our faith and not to bother. Having a biblically derived expectation of the future and the purposes of God surrounding our present-day witness is a massive help to us both individually and collectively.

Part of the crucial task of leadership (and the Ephesians 4 ministry of an evangelist) is to point God's people to what God has promised and to galvanise us into appropriate action in light of it. This avoids the extremes of hype or inertia from infecting the collective DNA of local church life or personal life. What God has promised will come to pass as we present ourselves willing ambassadors on Earth to do His will. We must do diligent exegesis on how we handle Scripture, that is to thoroughly and critically examine and interpret Scripture and then line up our practice and expectations with the certainty of God's promises.

The best days for the church lay ahead. Why do I believe this? The Bible convinces me this is a certain promise of God. It is not blind triumphalism, as we are for sure in a spiritual battle for souls, it is rather confidence born of careful exegesis. The one who promises is faithful. The Israelites standing at the edge of the Red Sea could hardly have expected it would part before them. But God had promised things that meant it had to. Likewise, we can hardly expect the cultural change in spiritual atmosphere in the West necessary for the gospel to take ground, but God has made promises that mean it has to happen at some point. It is right, on our part, to seek as individuals and as churches to be inspired, motivated, trained, seeking to stimulate a culture of 'everyone a witness' that becomes our part in preparing the ground for what God has promised to do.

God has done it many times before and will do it again. The Bible makes many promises concerning the fruitfulness of the church globally. Even with all the history of revival in many parts of the world we still have not seen anything that can be said to be the fulfilment of it. The tide has come in at various times and to various levels in various places but there yet remains the fullness of all that the prophets in the Old Testament. This is a huge motivation for our efforts. The tide is coming in; we may not yet see its fullness, but there is an inevitability to it.

> *It is evident from the Scripture, that there is yet remaining a great advancement of the interest of religion and the kingdom of Christ in this world, by an abundant outpouring of the Spirit of God, far greater and more extensive than ever yet has been. It is certain, that many things, which are spoken concerning a glorious time of the church's enlargement and prosperity in the latter days, have never yet been fulfilled.*

JONATHAN EDWARDS [43]

I believe, like Nehemiah, that God is building a city, a temple, but this time built without hands and stones. This new city is built of people, Jews and Gentiles, men and women; it is one new humanity in Christ, a glorious city on a

---

[43] Jonathan Edwards, 'An Humble Attempt To Promote Explicit Agreement And Visible Union Of God's People In Extraordinary Prayer For The Revival Of Religion And The Advancement Of Christ's Kingdom On Earth' in *The Works of Jonathan Edwards Volume 2* (Banner of Truth Trust, 1974), p. 278.

hill and a magnificent temple far outshining the one that came before.

God's purposes for His church are huge, therefore God's purposes in bringing vast numbers of men and women to Christ are a solid ground upon which to embark on our journey of seeking to stimulate a culture of 'everyone a witness'. I believe that rather than the church declining into near extinction and being overrun with the mark of the beast and the strength of Babylon, the Bible teaches us to expect that while the darkness will get darker, the light will also get lighter and not be overcome by the darkness but will rise and tower above it in the Earth.

Scripture boldly announces through Isaiah 2:1-3 (and restated in Micah 4:1-2):

The word that Isaiah the son of Amos saw concerning Judah and Jerusalem.

It shall come to pass in the latter days
that the mountain of the house of the LORD
shall be established as the highest of the mountains,
and shall be lifted up above the hills;

> *and all the nations shall flow to it,*
> *and many peoples shall come, and say:*
> *"Come, let us go up to the mountain of the LORD,*
> *to the house of the God of Jacob,*
> *that he may teach us his ways*
> *and that we may walk in his paths."*
> *For out of Zion shall go forth the law,*
> *and the word of the LORD from Jerusalem.*

At the other end of expectation is an over-realised eschatology whereby we think more of the fullness of God's kingdom has come into the present age than really has. This can cause significant discouragement over time as we seek results God simply has not promised at this time.

In this age, on this side of glory, not everyone will be healed, not everyone will turn to Christ, not everyone who shows signs of following Christ will stay true, not every mission will bring scores of people to Christ, not every church plant will survive. Sometimes, indeed many times as the present age progresses, we will have to learn to live with great mystery concerning turns of events that cause great perplexity and pain, setback, loss and sadness.

If we do not have a theology that allows for what we might see at first as a failure or even an evil apparently triumphing over God's good purposes, we will find ourselves in pastoral trouble. Rather than processing and lamenting our pain, whilst trusting relentlessly in the goodness of God, believers who subscribe to such a doctrine can often end up living lives of veneer and pretence. They 'confess victory' and refuse to consider anything but total kingdom success rather than processing pain with God, knowing He stands and weeps with us and is familiar with it.

He cried Himself over the death of His dear friend Lazarus. We live in the 'now and not yet'. Our theology must accommodate times of mystery, lament, disappointment and failure without us being completely derailed in our confidence in God or Scripture. I do not believe Scripture paints a picture of all-conquering triumphalism or invites us to live with the pressure of having to produce the fullness of the kingdom of God in each setting we engage with. "Salvation belongs to the Lord"[44].

---

[44] Psalm 3:8, echoed in Revelation 7:10.

Of the increase of his government and of peace there will be no end, on the throne of David and over his kingdom, to establish it and to uphold it with justice and with righteousness from this time forth and forevermore. The zeal of the LORD of hosts will do this.

ISAIAH 9:7

For he must reign until he has put all his enemies under his feet.

1 CORINTHIANS 15:25

Both of these verses capture wonderfully the ever-increasing, but not yet fully come on Earth, kingdom of Christ. More is possible than we have yet seen and it is on God's heart. We know how the story ends. Revelation 7:9 says, *"After this I looked, and behold, a great multitude that no one could number, from every nation, from all tribes and peoples and languages, standing before the throne and before the Lamb, clothed in white robes, with palm branches in their hands."*

I believe in the generosity of God's heart and that He wants us to catch that. He is not looking to make it hard for people, He is wonderfully patient and tender to all people.

> *The Lord **is** not slow to fulfil his promise as some count*
> *slowness, but **is patient** toward you, not wishing that any*
> *should perish, but that all should reach repentance.*
>
> 2 PETER 3:9 (EMPHASIS ADDED)

Hear that He wants 'all' to come to know Him. Revelation
shows it is not everyone who does, but it does show a countless
number.

'EVERYONE A WITNESS' – A FINAL THOUGHT

The harvest is plentiful. Jesus observed the issue is mostly to
do with the workers needing to be effectively equipped,
empowered and sent walking with Him.

We have a vision of big global purposes that Isaiah and the
prophets paint for us. Whilst typing this a very minor event
occurred. I paused writing to take my recently emptied
rubbish bin round the back of the house and stopped to speak
to one of our neighbours who has been experiencing some ill
health. During that conversation I said we would pray for their
health. We have and will and trust to build on these early
steps. It was just a small thing, a drop of water. But drop after

drop, after drop and what you end up with is an ocean. And an ocean tide that has gone out will surely come in again.

For the earth will be filled with the knowledge of the glory of the LORD as the waters cover the sea.

HABAKKUK 2:14

STUDY GUIDE

CHAPTER 1: ROCKPOOLS

Have you any experience of observing when 'the tide came in'?
Perhaps you've been in a nation where God was moving in a
powerful measure?

When you look at the state of Christianity in your area, is it
rock pools or tide coming in? And why?

How do the stories from Wales and Syria make you feel? What
do they do to your faith levels?

CHAPTER 2: TIME FOR THE TIDE TO TURN

Do you think Mike is too pessimistic in his assessment of the
current state of the western church?

Why might it be that the church in the global South and East is flourishing more than in the West?

In your nation and community what 'shakings' are you most aware of? How might God use these things to stir spiritual thirst amongst people for the gospel?

How does the concept of biblical lament make you feel?

Why are there very few modern lament songs?

How can we learn to lament well?

What stories hinting at a turning tide can you share today?

CHAPTER 3: READY AND EMPOWERED

How have you seen the pandemic change the openness to spiritual matters?

What is a better way to motivate ourselves than bulging eyes legalism and Spurgeon's challenge?

Can you describe being used for a divine appointment?

How can we overcome the fear of rejection?

How do we balance the difference between being ready to witness and feeling driven to witness?

Consider again the story of the church in Ukraine and the lady bringing her son to the church to receive prayer. What might make this kind of event happen with increased frequency in our own local church communities? What might draw people to seek your church out and ask for prayer?

Share a story of when you felt the Holy Spirit guided and empowered you to witness to someone... How did it make you feel? What was the result?

No one likes being rejected or feeling ashamed. What role does fear of rejection or shame play in holding us back from sharing our faith? How can we overcome this?

CHAPTER 4: COMMUNICATING THE GOSPEL

What do you think of the observation on the present day?

- 1950s to 1980s:

    Unchurched ⇨ Present Christ ⇨ Bring into church community ⇨ Join cause

- 1990s to 2000s:

  Unchurched ⇨ Bring into church community ⇨
  Present Christ ⇨ Join cause

- Current:

  Unchurched ⇨ Join cause ⇨ Bring into church
  community ⇨ Present Christ

How have you observed the different approaches for the different generations mentioned?

Do you think each of us naturally tends towards one of words, works and wonders? Which one resonates for you and why?

How can these three types of witnessing work together?

What is your personal 'sweet spot' in being a witness, words, works or wonders?'

What would your letter to the street be like? Anyone willing to do one and share it next time?

CHAPTER 5: CROSSING THE LINE

How would you tell your story of crossing the line? You may find it easier to think of two words that describe life before Christ, two words to describe coming to Christ and two words to describe life now and then build on that. Notice how everyone's stories are quite different. Spend some time giving thanks to God that you have come to know Him!

How do you detect spiritual thirst in those around you?

"One sows and another reaps"[45], how does that verse help us move from productivity-thinking to fruitfulness-thinking?

Make a list of as many ways you have heard of people coming to faith in Christ. Can you think of more possible ways that you and your church might be able to explore in the future?

---

[45] John 4:37.

147

CHAPTER 6: MATURE IN CHRIST

'Everyone a witness' must flow from hearts that want to tell others what Christ has done for them. Describe a time when you felt very stirred to witness, what was the cause of this?

How do we ensure we continue to be stirred to witness out of personal experience?

Sadly not everyone who comes to faith in Christ continues strongly in their faith. What do you consider to be the greatest challenges facing new believers today? How can we help them?

CHAPTER 7: COST, CLARITY AND CHANGE

Can you recall when God asked you to surrender something to Him? What was the effect?

What are the factors that might mistakenly cause the gospel to be viewed as an accessory to help us with life rather than a surrender to the Lordship of Christ? What can we do to avoid a consumer culture in our lives and churches??

Maturing in our faith is a process. What are the tools available to us to ensure we keep growing as believers? Where do the greatest challenges come from today in maintaining our witness and faith?

CHAPTER 8: THE GLOBAL PURPOSES OF CHRIST

Who's your 'one'? Who is the first person you are going to pray for until they come to faith?

Imagine our whole group or church did this? What would happen?

How can we as a group create a culture of 'everyone a witness'?

How does it make you feel knowing that God has made promises concerning the global scale of His purposes?

What's your take away from the book? What will you do differently from now on?

Begin the journey to sharing your faith regularly

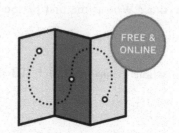

Take A Step

The Take a Step course helps small groups
rediscover the simplicity of evangelism,
one step at a time

relationalmission.org/takeastep

relational
mission

 #everyoneawitness